Walking the Cheviots

Classic Circular Routes

Edward Baker

Published by Sigma Leisure – an imprint of Sigma Press, Stobart House, Pontyclerc, Penybanc Road, Ammanford, Carmarthenshire SA18 3HP, UK

British Library Cataloguing in Publication Data
A CIP record for this book is available from the British Library

ISBN: 978-1-85058-488-9

Typesetting and Design by: Sigma Press, Ammanford, Carms.

Maps: Morag Perrott

Photographs: the author

Cover: Hexpethgate, looking east towards Cheviot

Printed by: Progress Press Ltd, Malta

Disclaimer: the information in this book is given in good faith and is believed to be correct at the time of publication. No responsibility is accepted by either the author or publisher for errors or omissions, or for any loss or injury howsoever caused. Only you can judge your own fitness, competence and experience.

Contents

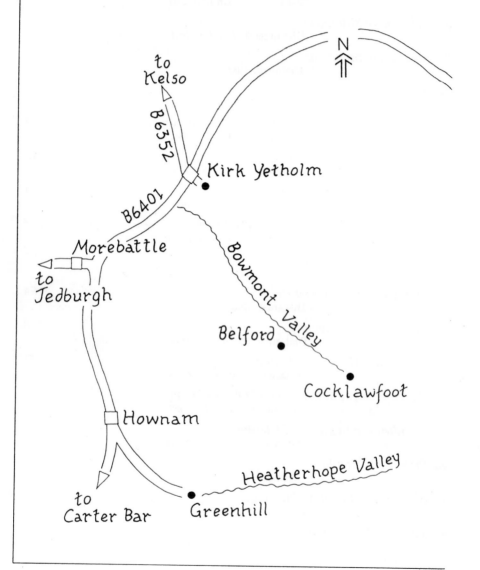

LOCATION MAP: Northern Cheviots

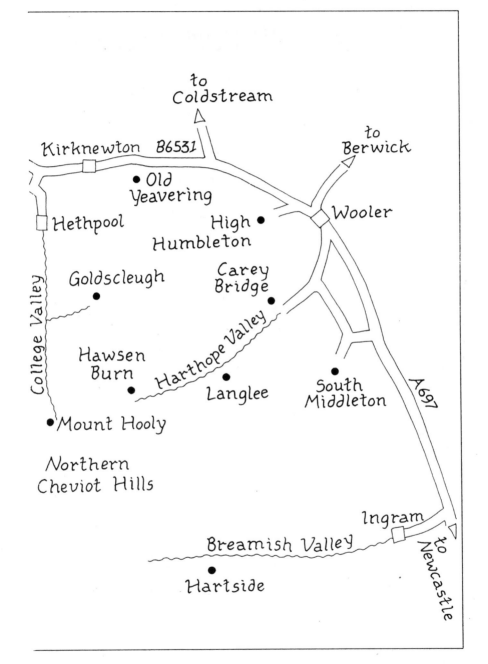

LOCATION MAP: Southern Cheviots

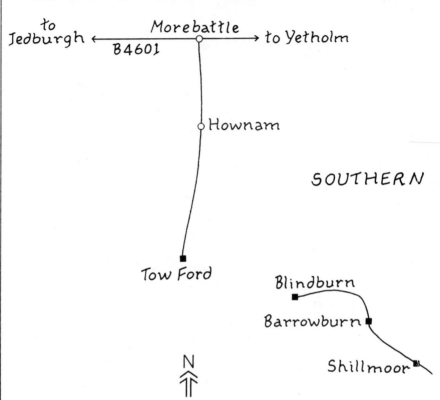

to Jedburgh ← ——— Morebattle ——— → to Yetholm

B4601

○ Hownam

SOUTHERN

■ Tow Ford

Blindburn ■

Barrowburn ■

Shillmoor ■

N
⇑

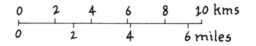

0   2   4   6   8   10 kms

0   2   4   6 miles

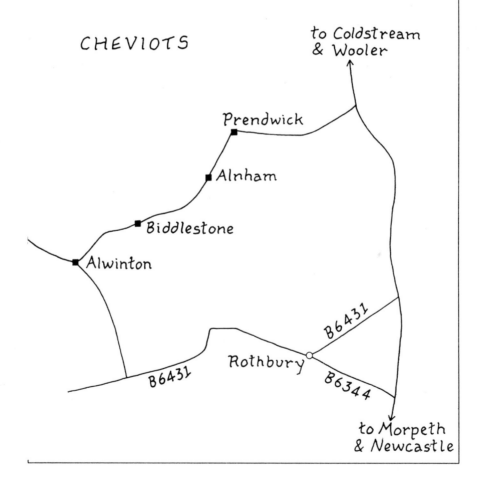

■ = Departure Points

CHEVIOTS

to Coldstream
& Wooler

Prendwick

Alnham

Biddlestone

Alwinton

B6431

B6431

Rothbury

B6344

to Morpeth
& Newcastle

The Cheviot Hills

The Cheviots are a paradise for walkers of all abilities. Unlike the crowded 'honeypot' areas elsewhere in Britain, this is one of the few places where you can find a combination of wild beauty, solitude (if that's what you want) and a warm welcome from friendly local people.

The hills themselves are rounded rather than rugged. They are, for the most part, covered in coarse grass, plus heather and bracken that add a glorious splash of colour on autumn days. On the poor and infertile soils, little thrives apart from sheep and these greatly outnumber their human counterparts. The Cheviot massif is the largest of the range and gives its name to it. Forestry has become an important activity in some parts of the region and you can also find occasional remnants of the old Cheviot forest.

Remote, wild and lonely, these hills are beautiful and have so much to offer. If solitude is your preference then the quieter areas can give you this in abundance. If you prefer the company of your fellow man then Breamish Valley with its open access on its haughland can give you all the family fun you could wish for. A lifetime would not give you sufficient time to explore these hills to their full extent. Take your time. Drink in the scenery, watch the wildlife, marvel at the quality of the air and appreciate the atmosphere of its pre-history. But please leave it as you find for the next one to follow in your tracks.

Walking in The Cheviots

In summer, these hills appear as benign giants, but appearances can be deceptive and many accidents occur each year because of walkers being lulled into a false sense of security.

On a summer's day, you can choose to travel light, with a minimum of supplies and foul weather gear: use an effective sun cream, wear a sun-hat and carry adequate water. Heat stroke can be just as dangerous as hypothermia. If mist draws in or conditions deteriorate, following a stream (a 'burn' locally) downhill will usually lead to a dwelling, but this may be a long way from your starting point, which means a long trudge back. One Cheviot valley or hill looks much like another in bad weather, as many have found to their cost.

In the winter, you would need full waterproofs, a change of clothing, extra food, gaiters and winter boots for even the shortest walk. Fatigue and cold are the greatest dangers to walkers. Wind, mist and snow or

rain are always worse with altitude and a calm cool day with a sprin-
kling of snow in the valley can be blowing a blizzard on the hill. Walkers
unprepared for the conditions they are likely to meet can end up
suffering from exposure or worse.

All walkers, and especially those new to hillwalking, should prepare
well before starting out. Wear clothes suitable for conditions and the
severity of the walk. Carry the appropriate map plus compass – and
know how to use it. Add reserve food and water to your pack – and most
of all, a smile and enthusiasm.

About the walks

All the walks described in this book are safe for the average, fit walker
and most are suitable for family groups. Dogs should always be kept on
a lead, especially during the lambing season which comes late in these
hills. Ewes are easily 'twitched' and a ewe heavy with lamb can easily
abort when frightened by a strange dog.

Remember that you are walking on private land and respect it as such.
Just as you would not appreciate someone walking into your house or
garden and telling you how to use them, the farmer does not appreciate
your comments on how he should manage his land.

Whatever your opinions on hunting, shooting or fishing we have the
ballot box in this country. Please leave your feelings at home. And if
you feel strongly about open access, join your local Ramblers Association group, but please do not badger the local people you meet. Common
sense and courtesy with compliance to the country code can do more
to enhance the reputation of walkers with land owners and improve
matters. Let common sense guide you.

Most of the walks in this book are on public rights of way, though
some use permissive paths. These are open to the walker at the discre-
tion of the landowner and can be closed at any time. Some walks use
stretches of high moorland which have been used by established
custom, such as Cheviot summit. Our freedom to walk is precious,
please do nothing to endanger it and keep to the Country Code.

About the book

This book is divided into two main sections, dealing with the Northern
and Southern Cheviots respectively. The first section describes walks
roughly north of the Breamish Valley, while the second section deals
with the southern hills and the Coquet Valley.

A suitable base for the Northern Cheviots is the market town of
Wooler. Alwinton is an ideal centre for the Southern Cheviots. Both
towns have an ample supply of guest houses and self catering accommodation.

Section 1:
The Northern Cheviots

The walks in this section are in the northern hills. Access to the walks is by way of five main valleys cutting deep into the heart of the Cheviots. These are the College, Harthope, Breamish, Bowmont and Heatherhope valleys. Walks are described that explore each of these valleys and there is an additional collection of walks grouped at the end of this section for those who have more time to spend in this attractive area.

Wooden duckboards on the Pennine Way

The College Valley

The valley was formed by a geological fault and glacial action. It is surrounded by high, rolling green hills, and is one of the most beautiful of the Cheviot valleys.

Little changed by the centuries, the scenery in winter has a wild grandeur with the contours of the hills etched in stark contrast by snow and frost. In spring, the broom and gorse clothe the valley in gold, followed by summer's voluptuous green. In autumn, the bronze of the bracken and autumnal leaves delight the eye. Through the centre of the valley meanders the College Burn, clean, fresh and cold from its source near the summit of Cheviot.

At the northern end of the valley stands the picturesque hamlet of Hethpool. There are many traces of early man from large hill forts to small settlements in this valley and, in a field just past Hethpool there is a prehistoric stone circle. The village nowadays consists of a single row of cottages with well-tended colourful gardens. Built in 1919 they replace the original farm cottages which formerly stood there.

Above Hethpool is Hethpool Bell, its sides covered with old gnarled oak trees. Planted by Admiral Lord Collingwood, whose wife owned a small estate at Hethpool in the 19th century, they were intended for 'navy timber', but they did not thrive and were never used. Today these woodlands form the residence of a multitude of wildlife including roe deer, red squirrel, woodpecker and insects too numerous to mention. In 1980 the trees were placed under the care and management of the Northumberland National Park.

The southern end of the valley is blocked by the Border ridge, separating England and Scotland. Before reaching this, you can see the highlight of the valley. To the left, just before reaching the ridge, is the Hen Hole, a massive gorge cut deep into the western flank of Cheviot. The College Burn has its birth in the Hen Hole and tumbles down in a series of pretty waterfalls. It is also the alleged home of the Northumbrian fairies.

Just beyond Hethpool there is a car park provided for visitors to the valley; from there, a private road leads up the valley. To preserve the unique nature of the valley, vehicular access along this private road is limited to twelve cars each day, and a permit is required. This is currently (2008) £10 per car and can be obtained from J. Sale & Partners, 18 Glendale Road, Wooler, Northumberland (Tel 01668-281611) by calling personally or by writing, and enclosing a stamped SAE. Those on foot can walk beyond Hethpool with no restrictions.

College Valley Estate: This private estate, extending to 12600 acres is owned by the Sir James Knott Charitable Trust. The estate consists of seven upland stock farms carrying Black Faced and South Country Cheviot sheep as well as cows. The land is all within the Northumberland National Park and rises from Hethpool at 128 metres to the summit of Cheviot at 815 metres.

Walk departure points

Hethpool: A visitors' car park is available just beyond the cottages and over the cattle grid (NT894283).

Goldscleugh: Limited parking on the grass verge of the road just before the buildings at Goldscleugh (NT914233). A permit is required to travel up the private road to Goldscleugh.

Mounthooly: Car parking is allowed on the grass land beside the gate leading to Mounthooly (NT882227). A permit is required to reach Mounthooly via the private road.

1. Mounthooly to the Hen Hole

This is a pleasant walk on good paths – non-strenuous and suitable for families.

Distance: 5.6km (3.5 miles)

Grade: Easy

Maps: Ordnance Survey Landranger 74. Ordnance Survey Pathfinder 475 NT82/92. Ordnance Survey Outdoor Leisure 16.

Start: At GR882227 next to the gate leading to Mounthooly.

The Hen Hole is a massive corrie and gorge cut deep into the western flank of the Cheviot. It was sculpted out by glacial action some 10,000 years ago at the end of the last Ice Age. The College Burn has its origin in the Hen Hole, tumbling down the gorge in a series of pretty waterfalls to flow out onto the valley floor. It is possible to venture up the entire length of the Hen Hole, but beware .. legend has it that this is one of the haunts of the Northumbrian fairies. It is said that, in days of old, passing travellers were often lured into the depths of the Hen Hole by the sweet sounds of magical music, never to return.

Pass through the barrier gate and along a made-up road leading towards the white bungalow of Mounthooly. Just before the bungalow take the rough track to the right. This leads, via gates, to the rear of the bungalow and the old farmhouse next to it.

The farm house was renovated in 1992 and is available as "bunk-house" accommodation, courtesy of College Valley Estates. Details and bookings can be made through the warden at Mounthooly, Tel: 01668-216358, or write to Mounthooly, College Valley, Wooler, Northumberland NE71 6TX for an information sheet. Accommodation can be provided for the lone walker and groups of up to twenty-five.

Keep to the track as it leads you up the valley. On the way you pass, via gates, the bottom edge of a coniferous plantation. After the plantation the track travels across open valley ground, passing native broadleaved trees planted in 1995.

In 1994, work began on the harvesting of trees from two plantations, later to be replanted with broadleaved trees. Just before the new plant-

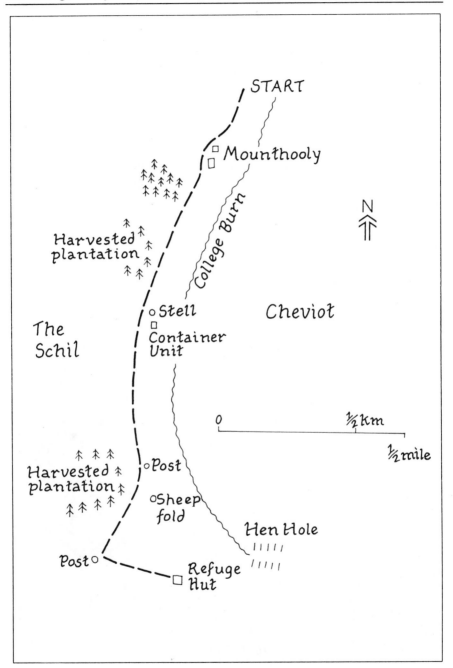

ing, there is an information board commemorating the clearing of the coniferous plantations and the beginning of the deciduous planting which will eventually forest the hills as they were many years ago. To your left is the College Burn with the Cheviot rising behind it, while to your right climbs the steep slope of the Schil. Looking ahead, you will see a deep red gash in the rise at the head of the valley. This is Red Cribbs, probably named after the colour of the soil here. In the Middle Ages it was known as Cribbheade. Local custodians of law and order described it as a well-used "byeway for the theefe". Most of the local population at the time indulged in a bit of 'shifting' (stealing stock and driving it across the border illegally in both directions).

Continue along the track to pass to the right of a stone sheep fold (called a "stell" locally) by a large white container unit. After some 100m from this point you will encounter a narrow stream running under the track, followed by another stream also running under the track just before the track bending sharply to the left.

Both streams carry drain-off water from the Schil into the College Burn. In Anglo-Saxon times the burn was known as "colleche", meaning "stream flowing through boggy land". The College Burn travels down the valley to flow into the Bowmont Water, a little to the north of Kirknewton.

The Hen Hole

Continue walking until you reach a point where the track divides, with a broad stone path leading off to your right. A public bridleway marker post is located to the left of this junction. At this point turn right on to the stone track until you reach a well-defined grassy path leading off to the left. Leave the track and continue along this path along the side of the valley until you reach a fork in the path. Take the left-hand fork. This leads towards the red scar known as Red Cribs and climbs the right side of the Cribs. When you reach the top continue straight ahead to a well-defined and used path with a marker post. To your left there is a wooden refuge hut.

****Other walks from Mounthooly start from here.****

The well-trodden path is part of the Pennine Way, a long-distance footpath stretching from Edale in Derbyshire to Kirk Yetholm in Scotland, a distance of 435km. The refuge hut was erected in 1988 by National Park wardens, Fell rescue teams and 202 Squadron from RAF Boulmer.

Turn left along the Pennine Way and walk to the refuge hut. The hut provides an excellent vantage point for viewing the Hen Hole.

At the time of writing this book, there is no public right of way to the Hen Hole, though by custom it has been walked. If in doubt, seek advice from J. Sale and Partners in Wooler.

2. Mounthooly to the Schil

An easy climb to the summit providing excellent views.

Distance: 8km (5 miles)

Grade: Moderate

Maps: Ordnance Survey Landranger 74. Ordnance Survey Pathfinder 475 NT82/92. Ordnance Survey Outdoor Leisure 16.

Start: At GR882227, next to the gate leading to Mounthooly.

The Schil lies north-west of Cheviot and, at 613 metres (1985 feet), fails by a mere 5 metres (15 feet) to achieve the distinction of being called a mountain. The top of the Schil, unlike the other Cheviot hills with their flat rounded tops, has a rocky pinnacle. On clear days, extensive views stretching deep into Scotland and England reward walkers for their efforts.

Go up the valley as described in the walk 'Mounthooly to the Hen Hole' – see page 6, until you reach the top of Red Cribs.

Turn right to continue along the Pennine Way, the Border fence on your left is now your guide and leads you up to the summit of the Schil. Due to the number of walkers using this path the surface has eroded badly; take care after a period of wet weather to avoid deep holes and water logged peat gullies. The last 100 metres to the summit is steep.

> The summit cairn of the Schil is located on the other side of the fence, in Scotland. It is best to cross the fence at the point where it bends sharp left near the summit. Perhaps a refreshment stop here would be beneficial where the spectacular views into Scotland and England can be fully appreciated at your leisure.

Return to the fence and cross back into England. Keep the wire fence to your left as you commence your descent from the summit and passing on the way some rocky outcrops on your right. The wire fence is later replaced by a stone wall. At a wire fence across the path, cross via the stile and continue to a ladder stile set in the stone wall, but do not cross over.

At this point the Pennine Way crosses the wall into Scotland and continues

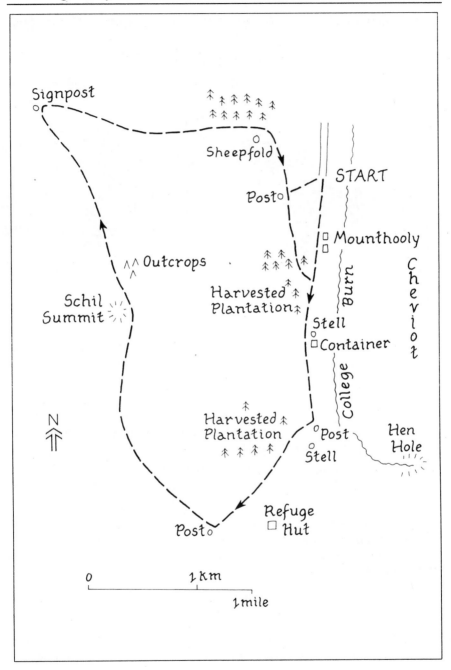

The summit of The Schil

on its way to Kirk Yetholm some 7.25km away. There is also a signpost bearing directions for Kirk Yetholm, Pennine Way, Mounthooly and the Schil.

Turn right, away from the stile, and follow an indistinct path over rough bracken-covered ground, marker posts aiding navigation. Bearing slightly right, the path heads towards a wire fence and reaches a gate with wooden foot boards underneath. Pass through and continue half-left over more rough heather moor, using marker posts as a guide.

> The path in the above section is not easily seen due to the rough nature of the ground. Walkers unsure of the way should head towards the right-hand corner of the coniferous plantation ahead.

The path leads to the right of the plantation and then runs parallel to it. Pass a stone sheep fold, which is visible slightly above and to your right. The path eventually curves to the right and leads down into the College Valley. At a gate, pass through.

There is an optional route here allowing you to turn left and descend to your starting point.

Continue ahead to a gate set in a wire fence. Pass through and walk on to the next gate which leads into a plantation. A short walk takes you through the trees to a gate allowing you to exit from the plantation. Turn half-left and down a grassy path.

Just after your exit from the plantation, there is a large circular depression on your right which is the site of an ancient settlement, one of many within the Cheviot Hills.

Turn half-left on reaching a wide track and follow it, passing to the rear of the bungalow at Mounthooly, to return to your starting point.

3. Mounthooly to the Cheviot

A good leg-stretching walk. It just has to be done. It is not advisable to attempt this walk in adverse weather conditions as Cheviot then becomes a very wet peaty bog.

Distance: 20.8km (13 miles)

Grade: Strenuous

Maps: Ordnance Survey Landranger 74 and 75. Ordnance Survey Path-finder 475 NT82/92 and 487 NT81/91. Ordnance Survey Outdoor Leisure 16

Start: At GR882227, next to the gate leading to Mounthooly.

The Cheviot, at 815 metres (2676 feet), is the highest mountain in North-umberland and gives its name to the range. Its summit is a disappointing broad plateau of peat hags with little to recommend it, but you have to do it just once. The approach, however, offers fine views in good visibility. It is best attempted after frost when the ground is then firm afoot.

Proceed up the valley as in the walk 'Mounthooly to the Hen Hole' – page 6 – until you reach the top of Red Cribs.

Turn left and follow the path of the Pennine Way as it passes to the left of the refuge hut and climbs steeply to Auchope Cairn.

Auchope cairn stands at 737 metres and is an excellent viewpoint with extensive views into Scotland. On a clear day it is claimed that, using binoculars, it is possible to discern the shape of Lochnagar, near Balmoral, some 160km (100 miles) away. With care you can approach the edge of the Hen Hole and obtain close views of its depths.

Pass Auchope Cairn and continue along the way, the going underfoot easier over wooden duckboards. At a wire fence, cross via the stile. A signpost bearing directions for the Pennine Way and Cheviot stands next to it.

The duckboards were installed during July and August 1981 by National Park volunteers The peat surface is very fragile and countless feet travelling along Pennine Way caused severe erosion.

After crossing the stile, turn left to commence the march to the summit of Cheviot. The path climbs parallel to a wire fence over Cairn Hill, on the way passing a large cairn of stones, known as Scotsman's Cairn to the right of the fence.

Mountain birds such as grouse, wheatear, golden plover and dotterel may be seen on the peat moors of Cheviot. Under foot may be found heather, ling, cotton grass, bilberry and cloudberry.

The way to the summit is one long plod across a flat plateau of peat, to a degree helped by stretches of stone slabs. The trig point, the latest of several which have sunk into the peat over the years, marks the summit.

The stone slabs were laid during 1993/94 to combat the erosion caused by the large numbers of walkers visiting Cheviot. On this section of the walk, take great care to avoid large holes and gullies in the peat. Walking can be hazardous at times after rain and no attempt should be made to the trig point in wet weather. Keep the wire fence within sight at all times, it is your guide and your lifeline if mist or low cloud suddenly descend to blanket the top of Cheviot, which often happens.

Continue past the trig point before descending a clear track. Take care as the going can be steep in places. The way levels out and crosses a saddle before making a gentle ascent of Scald Hill. Cross a fence using the ladder stile and continue over the broad grassy top of the hill and down the other side. At the foot of the hill, watch for a gate in the fence when crossing the saddle and, on reaching it, pass through.

Ahead and below stretches the Lambden Valley. During 1994 work began on the thinning of coniferous plantations in the valley. To your left rises Cheviot.

Follow the path as it makes a gentle descent towards the bottom corner of a plantation on the right flank of the valley. Enter the plantation through a gate and follow a broad fire break between the trees. Continue to a thicket of broom. The path passes through the broom and on to a gate allowing your exit from the plantation.

Keep alert and you may be lucky to see roe deer and foxes, which proliferate in this area.

Turn left after passing through the gate and follow a path parallel to a fence at the top edge of the plantation, eventually reaching a gate on your left. Pass through it and on to a path which leads diagonally down a heather-clad slope to join a broad well-defined track on the valley floor. At this track turn right and continue to a wire fence. Go through the gate and, a few steps on, pass to the left of a wooden sheep fold and a hut. Continue along the track to the next fence, cross via the stile and, keeping close to the burn, reach a wooden foot bridge. Cross the burn and ascend to the house and bungalow at Goldscleugh. Turn right on to a surfaced road which travels down the valley

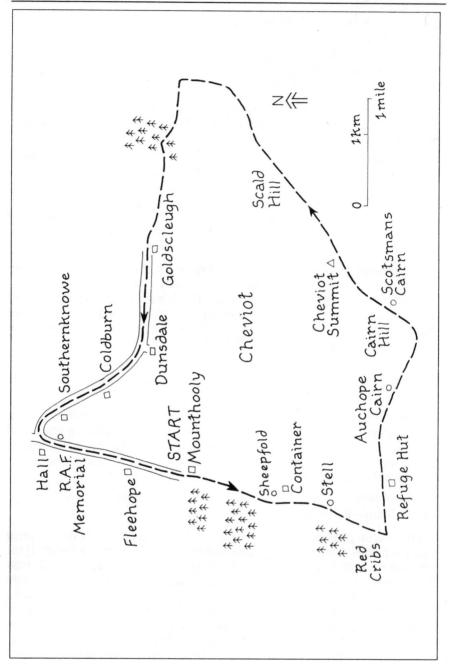

to pass the shepherd's house at Dunsdale; you finally arrive at Southernknowe, the last farm in the Lambden Valley.

In December 1944, during a late afternoon blizzard, a flying fortress of the United States Army Air Force crashed onto Cheviot. Hearing the explosion local shepherds Frank Moscrop of Southernknowe and John Dagg of Dunsdale accompanied by his border collie Sheila, set out to investigate. The dog Sheila found four airmen sheltering in a peat hole. Another three airmen found their way down to Mounthooly, the remaining two having being killed in the crash. As a result of their actions, both shepherds received the BEM, while Sheila the collie received the Dickens Medal, the animal equivalent to the VC. There is a public telephone box adjacent to Southernknowe.

After passing Southernknowe the road bends and dips to cross over a wooden bridge spanning the College Burn and enters the College Valley. After crossing the burn continue along the road to the College Valley Hall.

The College Valley Hall is used for regular dances and community activities. It is locally known as the 'Cuddy Stone Hall' because of its near proximity to the 'cuddy stone', a prominent boundary stone outside the hall. The hall contains photographs of the USAAF crash on Cheviot and illuminated addresses presented by the Air Ministry and the

Wreckage of World War II American bomber aircraft

USAAF commemorating the rescue. Incidentally, the covered doorway of the hall makes a fine refuge if caught out in a sudden shower.

Take the road leading off to the left and pass the RAF war memorial.

The RAF Memorial is dedicated to the wartime aircrews who lost their lives in the Cheviot Hills. It was unveiled by the Duke of Gloucester on May 19, 1995. Also present at the ceremony were Frank Moscrop, surviving aircrews and their families and the families of those who had died. A polished stone plinth lists the names of the 35 airmen who died in these hills, 1939-1945. Two seats are provided within the memorial for those who wish to meditate awhile. The stone walls of the enclosure were mainly built by 'Taffy' Nugent.

To continue, follow the road as it rises and contours around the side of Blackhagg Rig before descending to the farm buildings of Fleahope. Go through the farm, via gates, and continue along the road over Fleahope bridge to arrive back at your starting point.

4. Mounthooly to Windy Gyle

A leg-stretching walk with some bog hopping, but well worth it for the excellent views both along the way and, from the summit of Windy Gyle, a classic summit viewpoint.

Distance: 24km (15 miles)

Grade: Strenuous

Maps: Ordnance Survey Landrangers 74 and 80. Ordnance Survey Path-finders 487 NT81/91 and 475 NT82/92. Ordnance Survey Outdoor Leisure 16

Start: At GR882227, next to the gate leading to Mounthooly.

Windy Gyle, at 619 metres (2031 feet), is one of the higher mountains in the northern Cheviot range. A unique feature of Windy Gyle is the large cairn on the summit. A bronze age burial mound, it has in recent times become known as Russell's Cairn in memory of Lord Francis Russell, who was murdered in the summer of 1585 at nearby Hexpethgate during a March Wardens meeting. It is thought that the actual Russell's Cairn is slightly below and to the right of the summit. From the summit extensive views stretch into Northumberland, Tweedale and the southern Scottish uplands.

Go up the valley, as described in the 'Mounthooly to the Hen Hole' walk – page – 6 until you reach the top of Red Cribs.

At the top, continue straight ahead, crossing the Pennine Way and reaching a wire fence, the Border fence. Pass through the double gates in the fence into Scotland and on to Auchope Rigg. Descend the Rigg keeping a wire fence to your left. At a fence across the path at the foot of Auchope Rigg, go through the two wooden gates, ignoring a metal one to your right. Follow the path as it heads towards and around the base of a small hill. The path then leads towards the near top corner of the plantation ahead. Just before the plantation, pass through a gate in a wire fence. Head along the top edge of this plantation keeping next to a wire fence.

The coniferous plantations in the valley were established by the Forestry Commission. After the First World War, the country's supply of timber was seriously depleted and the Commission was set up to replenish the forests and generate a reserve supply of timber for future needs.

When the plantation ends, continue beside the fence to a gate. Go through and descend over rough ground to the Cheviot Burn, which you cross via a wooden foot bridge and turn right to Cocklawfoot farm. Pass through the farm and across the bridge spanning Kelsocleugh Burn. Your path continues straight ahead and up a small rise to a broad farm track. Turn left along the track and through a gate. Follow the track to the barrier gate of Kelsocleugh farm, but do not go through it.

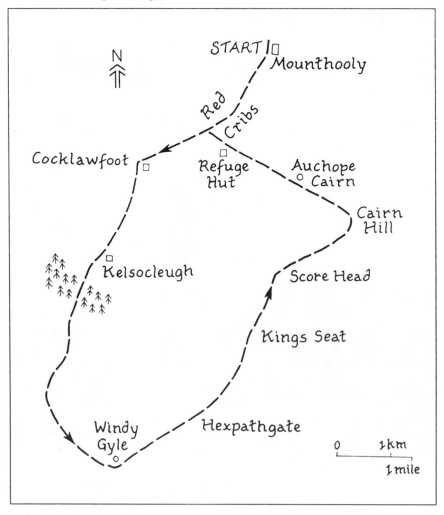

The Kelsocleugh Burn is a favourite haunt of the Dipper bird. This small black bird is easily identified by its white breast and short tail. It can frequently be seen sitting on a stone by the burn its head dipping at intervals,

Turn right and follow a grass path next to the stone wall. Ignore the gate in the wall and walk on a dozen paces to a ladder stile. Cross this then walk across the next two fields, via gates, to a gap in the plantation ahead. The path climbs through the trees to emerge on open land at the top of the rise.

Across the valley and slightly to the right, there is a fine view of Windy Gyle and much of the Border ridge. Cheviot is behind you.

Turn right and go through the wicket gate ahead. The path bends left and runs parallel to a wire fence to your right. The path later begins to rise and, where the fence turns right, leave it and continue half-left climbing a rise to skirt around the top of Kelsocleugh valley.

As you climb, the view into Scotland on your right opens up.

Cross a short stretch of open ground to meet a fence coming in from your right and, turning left, keep the fence to your right. Continue to where the ground begins to rise and begin your final approach to Windy Gyle. Pass by a stile in the fence and continue up the well-trodden path to where, after a short distance, a track leading off to the left takes you to the distinctive summit of Windy Gyle.

The summit is marked by a large cairn and an Ordnance Survey column. The cairn is on a Bronze Age burial mound. The views make the walk worth while, especially on a clear day.

To continue, walk south from the summit to a wire fence, the Border Fence. Go through the gate and turn left to follow the route of the Pennine Way. Cross a wire fence across the path, using the stile.

This next part of the walk can be a bit of a slog at times. Erosion has badly affected the ground, making walking difficult, especially after wet weather. To combat erosion, parts of this section have been paved with large flat mill stones by the National Park volunteer helpers and the results so far are excellent.

Continue for 2.2km to some gates set in the Border fence, and a four-finger signpost.

This is Hexpethgate, a recognised meeting place between the Lords Wardens of the Marshes. A signpost bears directions for the Pennine Way, Uswayford, Alwinton, Cocklawfoot, and Clennell Street.

Continue keeping to the Pennine Way route, passing over the broad tops of Kings Seat and Score Head and keeping the Border Fence to your left. After

Summit view from Windy Gyle

crossing the top of Score Head the path veers half-right and starts to rise towards Cairn Hill. Near the top of the ascent, wooden duckboards help the walker. These continue until a stile in the fence is reached, with a Pennine Way signpost next to it.

Again to combat erosion of the path, this length of duckboards was installed by the National Park Voluntary Warden Service during July/August 1981.

Cross the stile and continue over duckboards to the impressive stone cairns of Auchope.

It is said that these cairns were shepherds' cairns, where shepherds from the surrounding areas (such as Alwinton and the Beaumont valley) met to exchange sheep which had wandered off onto adjacent land during the year. On clear days the view is magnificent, stretching deep into Scotland. To your right is Hen Hole, a massive gorge cut deep into the western flank of Cheviot. A cautious approach to the edge enables you to peer into the depths.

Pass the cairns and descend on a steep incline until the ground levels out. To your right stretches the College Valley. The path then climbs a slope to pass by the wooden refuge hut. At a marker post turn right and follow the path down the left side of Red Cribs to a broad track. Follow this down the valley to return to your starting point.

5. Goldscleugh to Broadstruther

Easy walking, especially recommended for those seeking peace and solitude.

Distance: 11.2km (7 miles)

Grade: Moderate

Maps: Ordnance Survey Landranger 74 or 75. Ordnance Survey Pathfinder 475 NT82/92. Ordnance Survey Outdoor Leisure 16

Start: At GR914233 before the farm and bungalow

It is not advisable to attempt this walk in adverse weather conditions, such as heavy snow or thick mist, as the paths around Broadstruther are far from distinct.

Broadstruther, dating from 1689, was once a very prosperous farm; for some time it was an abandoned ruin but is now a renovated cottage. The main attraction for walkers lies in the solitude and silence to be experienced in the area surrounding Broadstruther.

Leave Goldscleugh by a small path to the left of the poultry shed and cross the Lambden Burn via a small wooden foot bridge. Keep the burn to your right and follow the path to a wire fence, crossing via the stile. Continue along a broad well-defined grass track to a wooden hut and a sheep fold, unusually built with wooden palings. A few steps on, pass through a gate in a wire fence.

The Lambden Burn has its beginnings on Cheviot and flows down the valley to join the College Burn just below the farm buildings of Southernknowe.

Continue along the path for some 200m, watching for a faint path which branches off to the left and rises up the side of the valley. Failure to locate this path could mean a steep climb later as the track peters out after passing a ruined sheep fold.

A good marker for the path is to observe that its beginning is directly opposite the end of the coniferous plantation, across the burn on the other side of the valley.

Follow the path as it climbs to pass between the gate posts of a fence which

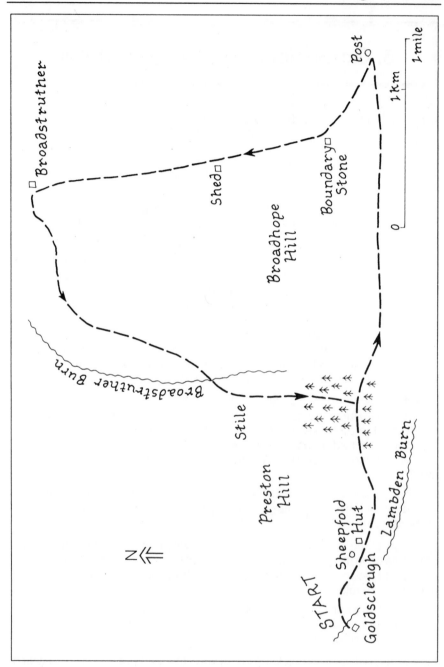

no longer exists. Take care as there is a considerable drop to your right and caution is needed as the path is eroded in places and can be slippy after rain due to sheep droppings. At the top corner of the coniferous plantation ahead, look for a gate in a wire fence.

During 1994, work began on the thinning of coniferous plantations in the valley.

Pass through the gate and bear right to follow the path as it borders the top of the plantation to another gate. Pass through the gate to a more recently-planted area. Go through a wicket of broom, deliciously fragrant when in bloom. Follow the path onwards down a broad fire break between the trees to eventually reach a gate allowing your exit from the plantation and on to open moorland.

Keep alert when passing through the plantation as you may chance upon some of the deer and fox which inhabit the area, plus the odd adder or two. The adder is Britain's only poisonous snake. Its venom rarely kills humans but can be fatal to smaller animals. It is easily recognised by the dark zigzag stripe running down its back and it is approximately 50-60 cm in length. The snake is found throughout the Cheviots and hibernates from October to late February.

The path rises gently up a bracken- and heather-covered slope to a wire fence with a gate. Pass through the gate and walk straight ahead over a grassy path. Ignore the strong path leading left to right after passing through the gate. The path leads you down a slope and then along the left side of the Hawsen Valley.

On descending the slope after the gate, note the reeds and wet ground to your right. This is the source of the Hawsen Burn which accompanies you down the valley on your right.

Continue down the valley till you reach a stone sheep fold. Some 350m after this, the path is joined by another descending from the left. There is a wooden marker post where the paths meet.

Looking down the valley the impressive crags of Housey Crags are visible against the skyline.

Turn left on to the path at the post and climb gently as the path rises to pass over grassy ground and then through heather. Continue to a gate set in a wire fence. Pass through the gate. Ahead and slightly left is a red metal shed. Head towards this and, on reaching it, pass to the right and up a slight rise. From the top, the buildings of Broadstruther are visible ahead. Make your way towards them, passing over some small burns and a deep gully on the way. Cross the farm boundary fence via the gate and on to Broadstruther.

Broadstruther provides an excellent resting stop. Take time to sit and

The Lambden Valley

enjoy the peace and silence. In windy or cold weather it will also provide some shelter from the elements.

Pass to the right of Broadstruther and then turn left to pass the front entrance and cross a stretch of open grass land to a wire fence. Pass through the gate and then head half-right. A narrow path leads you up a slope and then contours around the side of Broadhope Hill, before dropping to the Broadstruther Burn. Ford the burn and turn left with a wire fence to your right. Walk alongside the fence till you reach a stile. Cross over and turn left on a broad track and continue on this track to a gate leading into the plantation ahead.

To your left rises Broadhope Hill, to your right Preston Hill.

Pass through the gate and descend a forest path between the trees to a broad fire break crossing the path. Turn right here and up the fire break. Pass through a wicket of broom and through a gate a few paces on. Bear left along the top of the plantation and then through a gate to your left. Turn right on to a grass path to descend to the valley floor, where you turn right along a grassy track to return to your starting point at Goldscleugh.

6. Hethpool to Hethpool Linn

A pleasant short riverside walk, non-strenuous and ideal for families with small children.

Distance: 2.5km (1.5 miles)

Grade: Easy

Maps: Ordnance Survey Landranger 74. Ordnance Survey Pathfinder 475 NT82/92. Ordnance Survey Outdoor Leisure 16

Start: Visitors' car park just past the cottages at Hethpool. GR894283.

Hethpool Linn is a delightful waterfall approached through fragrant broom. As with all waterfalls it is best seen after a spell of wet weather. The walk continues to a quiet shady spot beside the banks of the College Burn. Ideal for a little contemplation accompanied by the music of the College Burn.

Hethpool Linn

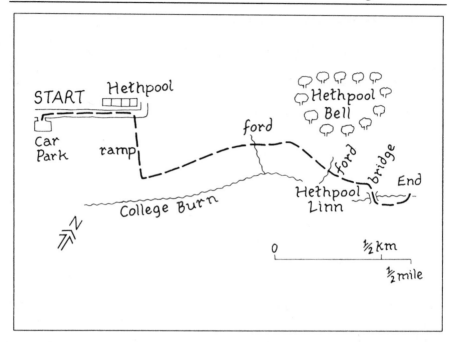

Turn right from the parking area, cross over the cattle grid and, keeping the stone wall on your right, walk back towards the cottages of Hethpool. When you reach a gate in the wall, signposted for Old Yeavering, pass through and along a broad track bordering a field.

> Built in 1919, the picturesque cottages replace the original farm cottages which once stood there. Records of Hethpool date from 1242, when it was known as Hetpol. In the Lay Subsidy Roll of 1296 some 18 persons were recorded as living there.

Continue along this track which develops into a concrete ramp as it descends towards a bridge spanning the College Burn. Before reaching the bridge turn left through a gate in the wire fence to your left to enter a small paddock.

> Ahead, and slightly to the left, is the oak-clad hill of Hethpool Bell. The oaks were planted by the famous sailor Admiral Lord Collingwood who inherited the Hethpool estate through his wife in the 19th century. The oaks were intended to be used as 'navy timber' but did not thrive and were never used. Roe deer inhabit these woods and can be best seen in the early morning or late evening when they descend to lower ground foraging for food.

Make for a gate in the stone wall at the other side of the field. At the gate, pass through and continue over rough pasture. Follow a narrow path to a plank bridge spanning a small stream. Cross over and, heading slightly right, climb the bank. The path continues right to a wire fence, cross via the stile. A few steps on, ford a small stream. The path at first runs parallel to a stone wall, later replaced by a wire fence. This angles away, leaving you to pass through the haughland of the College Burn, covered in fragrant gorse and broom bushes. A growing noise from the College Burn alert you to the presence of the nearby waterfall of Hethpool Linn.

A narrow track is seen to your right leading to a viewing area, where the falls can be seen to their best advantage. After taking your fill of the view, return to the main track. The College Burn flows into the Bowmont Water a little north of Kirknewton. The yellow flowers of the gorse appear all year, but are at their best from February to May.

At a fork in the track, turn right and descend to a gated wooden foot bridge spanning the College Burn. Cross the bridge, closing the gate behind you, and follow a path which climbs to your left to a wire fence. Cross via the stile and, beside an old oak tree on your left, descend to the wide gravel bank of the College Burn and relax.

Brown trout can often be seen leaping to catch flies, causing ripples in the water. Green woodpeckers are resident among the old oaks. Their cry, for all the world like laughter, frequently disturbs the peaceful surroundings.

To return, retrace your steps.

7. Hethpool to Eccles Cairn

A pleasant ramble with excellent views into Scotland from Eccles Cairn.

Distance: 12km (7 miles)

Grade: Moderate

Maps: Ordnance Survey Landranger 74. Ordnance Survey Pathfinder 475 NT82/92. Ordnance Survey Outdoor Leisure 16

Start: Visitors' car park just past the cottages at Hethpool. GR894283.

Eccles Cairn is believed to be the burial place of a prehistoric chieftain. Originally much larger, only a small cairn exists today as over the years stones have been removed for building material by local farms. From the cairn there are panoramic views into Scotland.

Leave the car park and turn right towards the cottages of Hethpool and, following the road left, go to a gate marked for Elsdonburn and Trowupburn. The main road to Westnewton leads off right at this point. Pass through the gate and follow the surfaced road until you reach a fork. Take the right fork and continue alongside a plantation to the farm buildings of Elsdonburn.

Elsdonburn is owned by College Valley Estates and is a stock farm with black-faced sheep and store cattle. The cattle kept on these upland farms, unlike those found on lowland farms, do not need to be housed during the winter.

The surfaced road peters out at this point and a rough track takes over leading you left up a short rise to pass the shepherd's bungalow of Elsdonburn. A few paces on the path swings right to pass through a gate marked with a yellow arrow.

A yellow marker arrow on gates or posts indicates a public footpath while a blue one shows a public bridleway.

Follow a broad track until a fork is reached. Take the path leading to the right and descend to the burn. Follow this path and cross the burn to a gate. Pass through the gate and along a rough track which rises gradually to pass along the side of a plantation. Pass through the gate through a wire fence. Turning half-left cross rough pasture, heading diagonally towards a plantation. Pass a sheep fold to your right. A gate is seen leading into the plantation.

This rough pasture is ideal for mushrooms and they can be found in abundance at the right time of the year.

Pass through the gate and turn left to follow a path between the trees, exiting via a gate at the other end of the plantation. Turn right and descend rough ground to a plank bridge spanning Tuppies Sike below.

The small stone building in the walled enclosure visible to your upper right was a 'shieling'. These simple dwellings were once used by shepherds staying out with their sheep during the lambing season. The advent of cars and tractors make their use today unnecessary.

Cross over the bridge and, turning left, look for a white topped marker post above and left. Walk towards this post, aiming for the small round summit visible between the two larger ones on the skyline. Other marker posts help you on the ascent. As the path levels, Eccles Cairn can be seen above to your right. The short climb to the cairn will reward you with superb views into Scotland.

Looking north, you may see the Lammermuirs; to the east, the three peaks of the Eildens; below, the Halterburn Valley, which leads to the twin townships of Kirk Yetholm and Town Yetholm. Evidence of Iron Age settlements and forts is also visible below.

Descend left from the cairn to the track below. Turn right and continue for a short distance to a stone wall with a wire fence adjacent, serving as the border between England and Scotland. The path runs alongside the fence and soon reaches a gate in the wall. Turn left here and follow a path leading away from this gate until you reach a fence across the path.

The path from the Border gate was known in the Middle Ages as the White Swire and was a well-used border crossing point. Maddies Well, some 500m along the path from the Border gate is the source of Tuppies Sike which flows down the valley to join the Elsdon Burn.

A gate allows passage through the fence to a path which contours around the side of Madam Law. A valley drops steeply away to your right.

Below, in the valley, can be seen the infant Trowup Burn. Later, it joins the Elsdon Burn to flow into Hethpool Lake and then into the College Burn. The word Law is from the Saxon 'hlaw' meaning hill.

After rounding the hill, the path leads over level ground. Watch carefully for a faint path leading off to the right. Good markers for this path are two large pointed rocks. The path passes to the left of them and descends towards the farm at Trowupburn.

In King John's reign this land, which was then called Trolhopeburn,

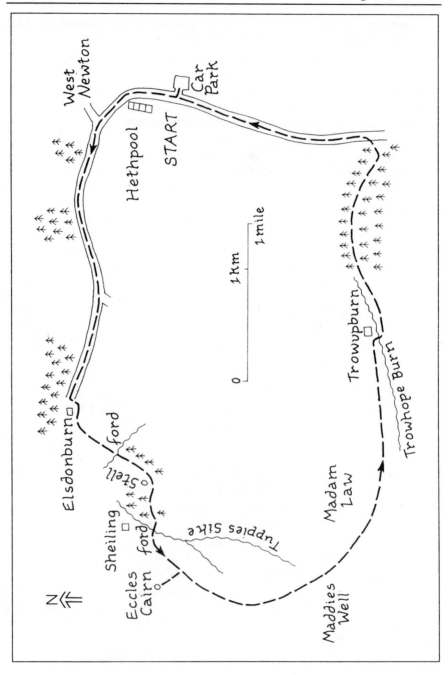

was given to the monks of Melrose Abbey by Robert Muschampe. Today it forms part of College Valley Estates.

Just before Trowupburn and across the burn to your right, can be seen a signpost bearing directions for Whitehall and Halterburn. Cross the burn and, following the directions for Whitehall, head diagonally up the river bank and on to rough pasture.

Trowupburn is worked as a stock farm by College Valley Estates and houses sheep and cattle.

The path leads past the front of the shepherd's cottage of Trowupburn and joins with a forest road leading to a gate into a plantation. Pass through the gate and along a forest road, eventually descending into the College Valley to meet a surfaced road. Turn left on this road and follow back to your starting point.

8. Hethpool to the Schil

A good leg-stretching walk providing some excellent views and ending with a relaxing walk down the College Valley.

Distance: 22.4km (14 miles)

Grade: Strenuous

Maps: Ordnance Survey Landranger 74. Ordnance Survey Pathfinders 475 NT82/92 and 487 NT81/91. Ordnance Survey Outdoor Leisure 16

Start: At the visitors' car park just past the cottages at Hethpool. GR894283.

The Schil, at 613 metres/1985 feet, provides excellent views on clear days encompassing Scotland and England. It fails by a mere 5 metres/15 feet to qualify as a mountain.

Proceed as in the 'Hethpool to Eccles Cairn' walk – page 30 – until you reach the gate in the Border wall.

Pass by the gate and continue by the Border wall. A short distance on the path contours around the top of a deep bowl to climb steeply up the slope of White Law. Cross a stone wall at the top using the ladder stile.

You have now crossed the border into Scotland. The dry stone walls found in the Cheviots are mainly of double wall design. Two outer walls are built tilting slightly inwards and the space between is filled with small stones.

Turn left and continue ascending, the wall beside you later being replaced by a wire fence. From the flat top of White Law continue to a point where this fence joins another and bends to the right. Turn right here and follow the path by it and make a steep descent from White Law. Now follow the path as it travels along the top of Steer Rigg. To your left is the Border fence.

The valley to your right is the Halterburn, leading to the village of Kirk Yetholm. The route you have covered forms part of the high level path of the Pennine Way.

After 1.5km, you reach a wire fence across the path. Cross using the stile and make a slight descent to a Pennine Way signpost.

The signpost is marked 'High Level', 'Low Level' and 'Pennine Way'.

The High Level route takes you along Steer Rig, while the Low Level route takes you along the Halterburn Valley.

Turn left at the signpost and follow the Pennine Way direction over a grassy path. At a fork in the path, take the left fork and continue to a track branching off right. Ignore this track and continue ahead to a stone wall which is crossed by a ladder stile.

This wall is the Border Fence, crossing the wall takes you back into England. A signpost next to the ladder stile bears directions for Kirk Yetholm, Pennine Way, Mounthooly and the Schil.

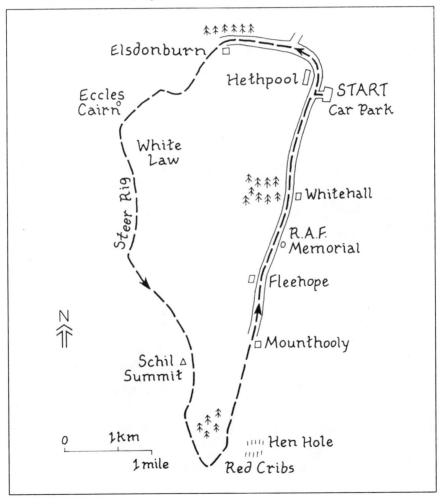

Turn right and, keeping the Border fence to your right, head on to a wire fence. Cross via the stile and start climbing as the path rises up the slope of the Schil. Pass by some large rock outcrops to your left and continue to the summit.

The actual summit cairn of the Schil is on the other side of the fence. The best spot to cross over is where the fence makes a sharp bend to the right before descending from the summit. Stop a while as you ascend the Schil, the views are stupendous encompassing as they do the whole of the Berwickshire coastline.

Following the fence, descend from the Schil and continue along a well-trodden path to a marker post. At this point turn left and follow a path which descends the left side of Red Cribs. At a broad track at the bottom continue along as it takes you down the length of the College valley to return you to your starting point.

Grey herons nest in the conifers opposite Mounthooly and they can often be seen fishing in the College Burn below the woods. It is Britain's largest long-legged bird with a length of 90-98 cm. They fish for the brown trout which are found in many of these fast-running mountain streams.

Returning via College Valley

The Harthope Valley

The Harthope Valley was formed on a geological fault line when the Cheviot range was created 380 million years ago. It was later scoured and shaped to the typical 'U' shaped glacial valley during the Ice Ages, the last of which ended 10,000 years ago. Down the centre flows the Harthope Burn, cold and fresh with brown trout darting about.

The Valley begins shortly after the oddly-named cottage of Skirl Naked. A narrow tarmac-covered single-track road drops very steeply from the cottage to the valley floor. A few hundred metres on, the road crosses a metal bridge spanning the Carey Burn, a major tributary of the Harthope Burn. This bridge was erected in 1956 to replace an earlier one which had been swept away by severe flooding in 1947.

The road continues, passing a coniferous plantation called Coronation Woods, which would suggest that it was planted in 1953. In 1995 work began on the harvesting of trees from this plantation, the intention being to replant with native broadleaved trees.

The road then passes between trees to a car park to the right of the road. A kilometre from here, the road passes opposite the farmstead of Langlee, situated on the opposite bank of the Harthope Burn. The road then winds on for another kilometre, finally reaching a bridge spanning the Hawsen Burn. It is here that the public access road ends.

Hawsen Burn was once named the Diamond Burn because of the beautiful quartz crystals to be found in its waters, though few remain today. Car parking facilities are available just before the bridge. From the bridge, a private road leads up the valley to the farm of Langleeford, sheltering amid a group of conifers. Cars are not permitted up this road but walkers are welcome.

It was at Langleeford in 1791 that the immortal novelist Sir Walter Scott, along with his uncle, spent a pleasant few days on holiday. By all accounts he found his stay enjoyable. The farm itself is on the opposite bank of the Harthope Burn, but no access is allowed.

Continuing up the valley, a broad stone track takes you along for 2 kilometres to the remote cottage of Langleeford Hope. Once the residence of a shepherd, it is now used as a holiday retreat. A grassy path leads onwards to pass Harthope Linn, a series of pretty waterfalls, and on to Scotsman's Knowe at the head of the valley which is the source of the Harthope Burn.

Wild life abounds throughout the valley and with luck and good timing you may observe fox, deer and badger. Hares and rabbits are also common as well as our only poisonous snake, the adder. Many birds of prey, including peregrine falcon and hen harrier can be seen in the upper reaches of the valley.

Walk departure points

Carey Bridge: Car parking is permitted on the grass verges to the right of the road just before the metal bridge spanning the Carey Burn at NT976250.

Langlee: There is a car park to the right of the road at NT951222, about one kilometre before the bridge spanning the Harthope Burn leading to Langlee.

Hawsen Burn: Car parking is permitted on grass land by the Hawsen Burn bridge at NT955227.

9. Carey Bridge to Old Middleton and Happy Valley

A pleasant walk ascending above a river valley and on to open hillside, returning via woodland and beside the river you saw below on your outward walk.

Distance: 7km (4.5 miles)

Grade: Easy

Maps: Ordnance Survey Landranger 75. Ordnance Survey Pathfinder 475 NT82/92. Ordnance Survey Outdoor Leisure 16

Start: At GR976250 before the bridge spanning the Carey Burn

This walk leads you across open farm land passing ancient settlements, an old abandoned village, a modern farm and returning by way of a mixed woodland bisected by the beautiful Coldgate Water.

Leave the parking area and turn right down the surfaced road to cross the metal bridge spanning the Carey Burn. Climb the fence to your left where it turns sharply left by the ladder stile provided.

The bridge spanning Carey Burn was erected in 1956 to replace the stone bridge which was swept away by floods in 1948. The abutments of the old bridge can still be seen to the right of the present bridge.

Follow the path, crossing the burn via a small wooden foot bridge, before climbing the steps cut in the slope ahead. From the top, turn left to continue along the path as it takes you along the top of the valley.

Coldgate Water flows in the valley below the old gnarled trees to your left. Further upstream this was the Harthope Burn, while downstream it becomes the Wooler Water. Many burns in the Cheviots undergo name changes on their journey to the sea.

Cross a fence via a stile then turn right to climb a steep rise away from the valley. The path soon dips to ford a small burn before climbing again to pass through a gate. At a wooden marker post turn half-left, passing two more marker posts. At an old stone wall the path bends left and descends back towards the valley.

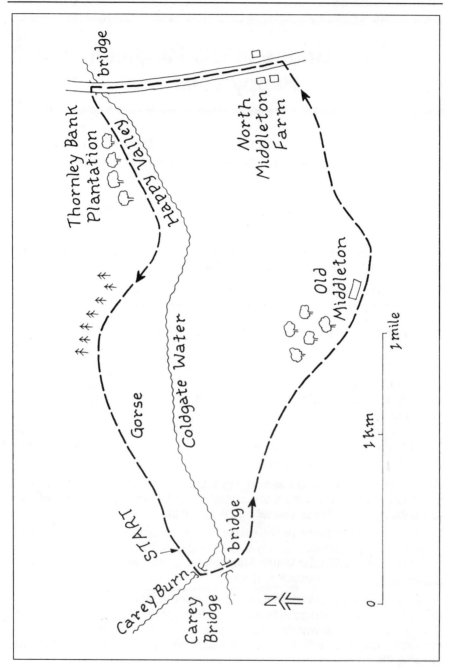

During this part of the walk there are some fine views of Northumberland. Rabbits abound on this hill side and if you are lucky you may see Mr Fox looking for dinner.

Continue along the path as it bends right and along the top of a small plantation. After the plantation the path skirts around the top of a deep basin dropping away to your left. Pass through a gate and continue to another; cross via the stile and turn half-left along the side of another plantation to a small wooden foot bridge. Cross over this bridge.

The foot bridge was built in 1979 by the National Park Warden, assisted by volunteer wardens.

The path climbs to a farm track. Turn right and, after a few hundred metres, arrive at the remains of Old Middleton.

Only the earthworks of this abandoned village are visible today. Originally it comprised of two rows of cottages north and south of a village green. In 1580 a Thomas Gray of Chillingham had eleven tenants living there. Today only a ruined shepherd's cottage marks the site. These abandoned villages are often the result of farm mechanisation causing a drop in required manpower, resulting in rural depopulation.

After contemplating on the nature of things, retrace your steps and return to the track. Pass through a gate set in a restored stone wall. A plaque in the wall reads 'Arres and Son, Kelso, 1986'. They can be justly proud of their work.

The ford at Coldgate Mill

Continue onwards following the farm track as it gently descends to join a surfaced road. Turn left along the road and pass between the well-kept farm buildings of Middleton farm and Middleton House. After a half kilometre the road dips to the Coldgate Water ford.

It is here that the Coldgate Water changes its name to the Wooler Water.

Cross the burn using the metal bridge to the left of the road. Once over the bridge, pass through a kissing gate and turn left to enter the patch of mixed woodland known as Happy Valley.

This is a delightful and pleasant woodland walk, with the Coldgate Water tumbling through. A walk of beauty to delight the walker. Happy Valley was probably christened by the ladies of nearby Middleton Hall who often walked this way during the last century. The walk is especially beautiful in spring when primrose and other early flowers are in bloom, though autumn colour also holds its own attraction.

The woods run alongside the Coldgate Water before a gate leads to open valley pasture.

The wood is Thornley Bank Plantation, offering a woodland walk of rare beauty. The plantations along the valley are privately owned and used for rearing game birds. The open valley pasture is Grimping Haugh.

The path crosses open land to a fence, crossed via a stile. It continues to the left of a plantation and over open land dotted with gorse bushes. Soon the path rises to the right and winds along a gorse-covered slope. The path at this point is narrow but distinct. The path then descends to ford a small burn and continues over haughland to a fence. Again cross using the stile then walk on to the final fence. Pass through a gate on to a surfaced road and turn left to return to your starting point.

10. Carey Bridge to Broadstruther

An easy climb at the start with fairly level ground afterwards.

Distance: 8.6km (6.3 miles)

Grade: Easy

Maps: Ordnance Survey Landranger 75. Ordnance Survey Pathfinder 475 NT82/92. Ordnance Survey Outdoor Leisure 16

Start: At GR976250 next to the bridge spanning the Carey Burn.

Broadstruther was once a prosperous farm, dating back to 1659. It eventually became an abandoned old steading but, in 2007, it underwent extensive renovation. The attraction of this walk lies in its quiet and solitude.

Leave the parking area and cross the bridge spanning the Carey Burn. On the other side there is a signpost to your right marked 'Broadstruther 2.5 miles'. Climb up the stone track as indicated by the signpost to pass to the right of a large cattle shed and reach a gate.

The present Carey Bridge was built in 1956 to replace an earlier one which had been swept away in floods. The abutments of the old bridge are to the right of the present bridge.

Go through the gate and continue along the track to another gate. Pass through and continue along the right-hand side of a plantation then, keeping on the track, continue to climb the lower slope of Snear Hill.

As you ascend, look back and admire the view. The higher you get, the more expansive the view towards the North Sea. The red sandstone rim can be clearly seen, as can the distinctive hump of Ros Castle on the horizon surrounded by a mantle of trees.

Ros Castle is not a castle as such but an Iron Age stone fort sited on the top of the hill. It provides an excellent viewpoint for the whole Cheviot range.

The ground levels as you pass through a gate following the track as it contours the lower slope of Snear Hill. Pass to the left of some old derelict sheep pens ignoring a lesser track leading off to the right. Continue to a gate set in a fence running across the track. Pass through and continue ahead.

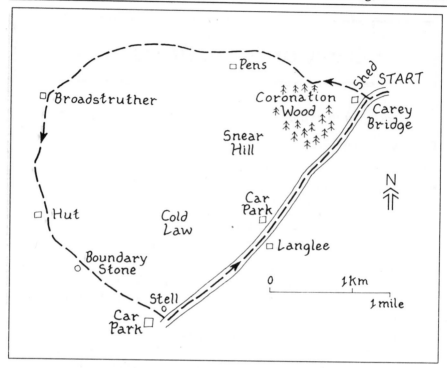

Eventually, as the track curves to the left, the buildings of Broadstruther are seen ahead amid a small cluster of trees in a large bowl-shaped depression.

Keep on the track until you reach a wooden marker post with a yellow arrow. Turn half-right as indicated and cross rough ground towards a stile in a fence ahead. Cross the stile and walk straight on to the next marker post. This is positioned to the side of a wide track.

This track provides easy access to the shooting butts on the hillside. The heather moors hereabouts are managed for game bird shooting.

Cross over the track and on to rough ground to a tractor track. Follow this down to the Hazelly Burn. Cross the wooden foot bridge. Turn left and follow a path leading up and out of the gully to a gate above. Pass through the gate and continue ahead, passing through gaps in two derelict stone walls, to Broadstruther.

Time for a refreshment stop to relax and enjoy the atmosphere of the place. The walls of Broadstruther will provide shelter from the winds while the trees will shade you from the sun.

The ruins of Broadstruther prior to its renovation

To continue, walk from the buildings to the track which runs past the ruins. Turn right on to the track and go forward to a blue marker post. Leave the track here and follow the directions indicated to a gate in a wire fence. Go through the gate and across the field to the next gate. Pass through and turn left towards a wooden pole visible next to a grassy path on the small rise ahead. A few paces from the gate you will cross a deep gully.

Aim for the saddle between Cold Law and Broadhope Hill ahead, behind which is visible the cone-shaped summit of Hedgehope Hill. Any route difficulties found in following the above directions may be overcome by doing just this, being careful to avoid any deep gullies or holes when the ground is snow-covered.

From the wooden pole, continue along an indistinct grass path, later passing to the left of a corrugated iron shed. The path traverses heather moor. After passing the shed and crossing a deep gully, follow the path as it climbs the heather-clad slope, eventually reaching a wire fence and a gate at the crest of the slope.

To the right of the gate there is a boundary stone. One side bears the letter S while the other side bears the letters SH.

Pass through the gate. Ignore the well-trodden track to your left and right. Continue straight ahead on a lesser path through heather and bracken.

Further on the heather and bracken disappear and the path leads over short grass to descend into the Hawsen Valley. Walk along the path as it contours the middle slope of a valley, passing a wooden marker post to the right of the path. Continue onwards to a stone sheep fold above a tarmac road. At this point descend to the road and turn left. This road takes you along the Harthope Valley and back to your starting point.

This road is usually quiet, so you still enjoy the beauty of the valley – except on Bank Holidays.

11. Langlee to Old Middleton and Threestoneburn Wood

After a short climb, the route levels out and is fairly level most of the way; a gentle descent ends the walk.

Distance: 13km (8 miles)

Grade: Moderate

Maps: Ordnance Survey Landranger 75. Ordnance Survey Pathfinder 475 NT82/92. Ordnance Survey Outdoor Leisure 16

Start: At GR951222, car park 1km before Langlee bridge.

Old Middleton: Only the earthworks remain of this abandoned village. A ruined shepherd's cottage marks the site. Some fine examples of hut circles can be found in the area.

Threestoneburn Woods: One of the larger plantations within the Cheviots. It also contains the remains of a prehistoric stone circle.

Turn right away from the car park and walk down the surfaced road for approximately one kilometre to a signpost to the left of the road. This bears directions for Middleton Town and N. Middleton. Use the stile next to the post to cross over the wire fence. Continue to a bridge spanning the Harthope Burn. Cross the burn and turn left up a stone track towards the buildings of Langlee. Just before reaching them, a white arrow directs you to the left. Follow the fence around the front of Langlee. Once past the steading a grass path makes a steep ascent out of the valley up the slope of Brands Hill.

As you climb, admire the view as you see the valley unfolding below. Looking back, you should see the white house of Langleeford amid a cluster of trees in the middle distance. The view continues to the head of the valley at Scotsman's Knowe, with Cheviot to the right.

The ascent is steep at first, but eventually becomes less arduous. When you reach a marker post continue straight ahead as shown by the yellow arrow. Ascend a small rise and reach a wire fence, cross via the stile. Remain on the path to the next marker post.

At this marker post look to your right and note the large stone walled

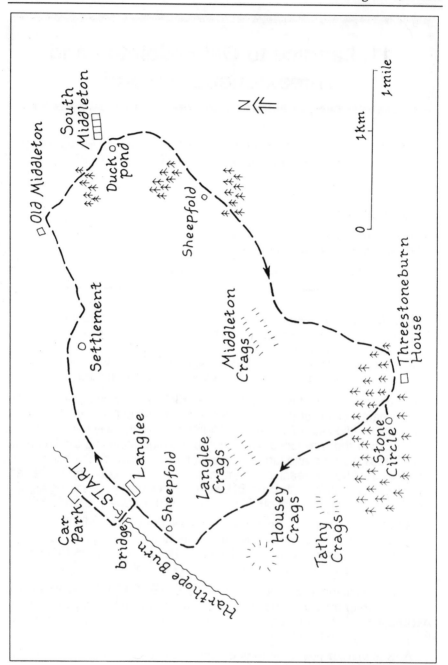

The Harthope Valley

enclosure. This was once an ancient homestead, a field system is located near to it.

Continue past the marker post as indicated by the yellow arrow. Soon the path begins to make its descent from Brands Hill. At a wire fence, cross the ladder stile to the left of the gate. Sheep pens are visible to your right. Follow the path keeping a wire fence to your right.

When you reach the point where the path and fence bend half-right, look to your left and notice the mounds of stones in the field. This is the site of an ancient settlement.

Climb the ladder stile over a fence and continue with a dry stone wall to your left. At the next fence, cross the stile. Ahead, there is an old abandoned cottage. Remain on this path till you reach this ruin.

This is the site of Old Middleton. Originally two rows of house stood here to the north and south of a village green. In 1580 there were eleven inhabited dwellings here. Some fine examples of the remains of hut circles may be seen easily discernible as grassy mounds to the right of the track.

Continue on the track, leaving behind you the old town. At the point where the track makes a sharp turn to the left leave the track, turning right, to follow a grass path which leads to a stone wall. At this wall, cross via the stile. Turn left and walk parallel to a wire fence. At the point where the fence bends to the left leave the fence and turn right, up a slope to the left corner of the plantation ahead.

There is a public footpath but the path is not visible on the ground. Please follow the line of the path across the field towards the plantation ahead.

At the corner of the plantation, which is enclosed by a dry stone wall, pass through the gate leading into it. A good path will take you through the trees. Keep the stone wall on your left until you reach a wire fence marking the boundary of the plantation. To the right a stile enables you to cross the fence. Turn half-left and continue over a grass field to South Middleton. At a farm track turn left and through the gate. Continue past the left of a duck pond and reach a signpost to the right of the road bearing directions or Threestoneburn and the Dodd.

The duck pond is often inhabited by a variety of ducks, geese and moor hen. If you have any bread or tit bits to spare, they will provide welcome entertainment.

Turn right at the signpost and along a stone track to a fork in the track. Take the right fork soon reaching a stone wall crossing the track. Go through the gate and ascend slightly to pass to the left of a plantation. Just before another stone wall the track turns left, continue on the lesser path to the right and in a few paces reach a stone wall. Cross over it using the ladder stile.

There are two arrow indicators on the stile the one pointing left leads to the cottage of South Middleton Moor. We follow the one ahead.

After crossing the stile, turn half-left on a grassy path to pass to the left of a stone sheep fold and through a gate in a wire fence. Now turn half-left and head towards the plantation ahead.

Looking to your left and slightly ahead you can see the distinctive outline of Middleton Crags set against the sky line.

From the plantation, a stile leads into the trees. A yellow arrow indicates direction. Continue to a hollow and another stile in the fence surrounding the plantation. From this stile, climb up and out of the hollow to another stile set in the fence above. Cross over and turn half-right to a wooden marker post next to a good farm track. Turn left on to the track to a gate. Pass through and continue along the track which rises gently up the lower slope of Middleton Crags and then curves to the left around its base.

The grassy land to the left of the track is the home of the wheatear. It is one of our earliest visitors arriving towards the end of March. It can easily be distinguished by its undulating flight and flashes of white on its wings.

Leave the track where it turns sharp right to climb to the crags and continue on a less distinct path. Pass through the gate in a wire fence and walk to a large coniferous plantation. A gate allows you to enter the trees.

This is Threestoneburn Woods, one of the larger plantations within the Cheviots. There is more land covered by trees in this country than at any other time in the past thousand years. However, while coniferous trees are abundant, it is sad to note that oak and hazel are now dying off quicker than they are being reproduced. In time, without man's help, they could eventually become extinct.

A broad heather-lined track leads between the trees to exit by a stile in the wire fence ahead. After crossing the stile, walk on a few steps to a forestry road and a marker post. Turn right and through a gate and continue down the track to Threestoneburn House.

Threestoneburn House was once a shooting lodge but now is a holiday retreat.

The track leads to the right of the house and on to a wooden bridge spanning the Threestone Burn. Cross the bridge and bear half-right as shown by a blue arrow. Walk across the grassy path to pass through a gate in a wire fence, then cross another foot bridge and continue to a stone wall.

These wooden foot bridges were built by National Park voluntary wardens in 1989.

Pass through a gate in the wall and turn left. Ford a small burn and continue to site of Threestoneburn stone circle.

The circle is believed to have been used for ceremonial occasions. Of the thirteen original standing stones only three remain upright, the remainder lie scattered around. A flint knife found during excavations is on display at the Museum of Antiquities, Newcastle Upon Tyne.

Retrace your steps back to the gate in the stone wall and turn left to follow a path up a short rise through the trees. Keep to the path until you reach a broad fire break running left to right, continue straight ahead. Eventually this path leads to a gate allowing you to exit from the trees and on to open heather-covered land.

On the left are the twin outcrops of Tethay Crags, while ahead are Langlee Crags. To your right are Middleton Crags and, immediately right, the hump of Steel Crag.

Walk straight ahead from the gate for 50 metres to a well-defined grassy track. Turn left and follow it across heather to pass to the right of a hut and up a small rise. The column of Housey Crags becomes visible to your left. The track passes between Housey and Langlee Crags before descending towards the Harthope Valley. A wire fence approaches from the right and runs parallel to the track. This becomes a stone wall; leave the track and pass through a gate in the wall. Once through, turn left and descend, keeping near to the stone wall on your left.

The descent into the valley is a highlight of this walk. The view along the valley is exceptional while, beyond, is the Northumbrian coastal plain.

Remain near the wall till you encounter a marker post. Turn right and continue descending to pass to the left of a sheep fold. Climb the small rise and follow the path to a gate. Pass through and descend to the bridge spanning the Harthope Burn. Cross over and on to a wire fence. Cross via the stile and turn right along the road to return to the start of your walk.

12. Hawsen Burn to Cold Law

An airy walk with an easy ascent and a return down the Harthope valley. Please note – this entire walk is over permissive paths and is currently being renegotiated. Walkers should contact Lilburn Estates (Tel. 01668 - 217331) for current information.

Distance: 6.5km (4 miles)

Grade: Easy

Maps: Ordnance Survey Landranger 75. Ordnance Survey Pathfinder 475 NT82/92. Ordnance Survey Outdoor Leisure 16.

Start: At GR955227 before bridge spanning the Hawsen Burn

Cold Law at 452 metres provides some really excellent views over the Northumbrian coastal plain. It will amply repay the limited effort to reach its summit.

Walk towards the stone sheep fold on the right of the Hawsen Burn parking area beside the National Park map and information board. Climb the rise behind it to a distinct path. Turn left along this path and up and along the side of the valley.

At a fork on the path turn left and continue onwards, keeping above and to the right of the swiftly flowing Hawsen Burn below you. At another fork in the path, with a wood marker post, take the right-hand path marked by a blue arrow. The path rises over heather and bracken to a gate in a wire fence.

This gate leads over an indistinct path to the buildings of Broadstruther farm.

> To the left of the gate stands an old boundary stone. These were used to mark boundaries between adjacent land owned by separate landlords or parishes.

Ignore the gate and turn sharp right to ascend a distinct path to the summit of Cold Law. Keep parallel to the wire fence on your left. The last 100 metres are steep, with occasional granite outcrops.

> This path is well-used and as a result the surface has eroded, exposing the peat below. After periods of wet weather the ground can be squelchy. As you ascend, the view to the left opens to reveal the buildings of Broad-

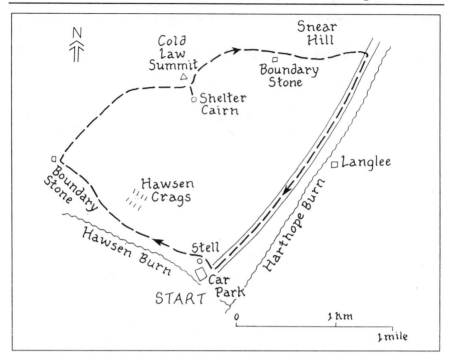

struther set amid a clump of trees. On gaining further height the view into Scotland gradually opens up.

At the summit, turn right and make your way towards the Ordnance Survey column.

With the arrival of satellite technology, these trig points are now sadly obsolete. Some have been adopted by walkers' groups who have made themselves responsible for their maintenance.

Continue past the survey column on a narrow path through the heather to an impressive shelter cairn overlooking the valley.

This shelter is an ideal spot to enjoy the extensive view sheltered from the weather. Across, half-right, rises Hedgehope Hill and further round to the right the bulk of Cheviot dominates the skyline. Looking left the view across Northumberland to the coast is stupendous.

When you are ready to depart return to the survey column. Look to your right and locate a marker post. Continue towards the post then descend a short slope to the next marker post. Cross the heather moorland (gorgeous in August) guided by more marker posts, towards a broad green track visible on the hill side ahead.

The summit of Cold Law

At a wire fence, go through the gate and turn half-left to pass to the left of a boundary stone similar to the one beside the gate leading to Broadstruther. Follow the broad track to descend to the valley floor. Turn right along the tarmac road and follow it to return to your starting point.

13. Hawsen Burn to the Cheviot

A strenuous walk, offering the opportunity to stretch your legs and exercise your lungs.

Distance: 14km (8.8 miles)

Grade: Strenuous

Maps: Ordnance Survey Landrangers 75 & 80. Ordnance Survey Pathfinders 475 NT82/92 and 487 NT81/91. Ordnance Survey Outdoor Leisure 16

Start: At GR955227 beside the bridge spanning the Hawsen Burn

The Cheviot is a must for walkers in the area. It is a walk one just has to do. At 815 metres (2676 feet) it is the highest summit in Northumberland, giving its name to the whole range.

Go behind the stone sheep fold to the right of the parking area and climb the small rise to a well-worn path. Turn left and follow the path as it contours the slope above Hawsen Burn. Ignore any sheep tracks or paths leading off right until you reach a fork in the path with a small wooden marker post bearing blue and yellow arrows.

Looking behind, the distinctive shape of Housey Crags can be seen across the Harthope Valley. These were formed 380 million years ago shortly after the area underwent a violent phase of volcanic activity forming the Cheviot range. Above and to your right, are Hawsen Crags which were formed at around the same time.

Turn left as shown by the yellow arrow. The Hawsen Burn flows on your left. Pass to the left of a sheep fold and continue, as the path rises, to a wire fence and a gate. Do not pass through the gate.

This gate leads into the Lambden Valley and Goldscleugh. Above and to your left can be seen the northern flank of Cheviot, your ultimate goal.

Turn left and, keeping parallel to the fence, follow the path as it ascends Scald Hill. On the way, cross a fence running across the path via the stile. Transverse the broad flat grass top of Scald Hill then descend to the coll, crossing the next fence by the stile. Ahead lies a short stretch of level ground

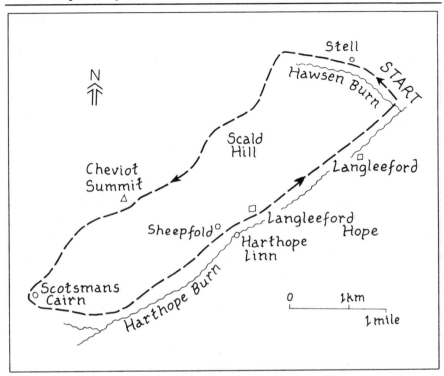

before the ascent of Cheviot. This is the point to gird your loins for the steady climb ahead.

While climbing Cheviot, pause to admire the view both to your left and behind you. The view on the ascent for exceeds the view from Cheviot's vast peaty plateau. On clear days it is possible to see the entire panorama stretching from the Lammermuirs to Tynemouth.

Though at times you may doubt it, eventually you will reach the top. The Ordnance Survey column marking the actual summit is reached over a flat peat bog. The wire fence next to the path is a safe guide across this lunar-like landscape.

During the crossing of Cheviot always keep the fence within sight. It is your guide across and your lifeline if mist or low cloud suddenly descend and blanket the area, as so often happens in these hills.

The Ordnance Survey column is located to the right of the fence surrounded by soggy, muddy peat — a veritable quagmire after wet weather. Do not attempt to reach the column after heavy rain, horses have been said to disappear in this peat bog.

Cheviot Summit

Peat bog develops when the ground becomes waterlogged due to poor drainage over impermeable granite. The anaerobic conditions thus produced do not allow the complete breakdown of dead vegetation. The material gradually builds up, causing wet acidic conditions where few plants can survive. Typical vegetation being heather, bilberry, cloudberry and cotton grass. Sundews are also present: carnivorous plants that obtain nitrogen from their prey. Sphagnum moss also thrives in these conditions.

Continue past the column, keeping next to the fence as before.

The Ordnance Survey column is mounted on concrete blocks placed one on top of the other as their predecessors gradually sink into the peat. At the time of writing, the latest concrete block was installed on the 21st July, 1993. To combat erosion of the path across Cheviot, stretches of large stone slabs have been laid by National Park voluntary wardens allowing safe access for walkers.

After a steady descent, you climb again. After crossing Cairn Hill, the path descends past peaty lakes to your left to a large stone shelter on the other side of the fence. This is Scotsman's Cairn. Cross via the nearby stile and head towards the cairn, continuing past and beginning the descent into the Harthope Valley.

There is no obvious path over this rough ground; choose the easiest descent available utilising sheep tracks where possible – sheep do not like wet feet either. Near the bottom you will encounter a marshy area and a small trickle of water, this is the start of the Harthope Burn.

Follow the embryonic stream as it flows to your left and continue down into the valley. At first there is no distinct path and you will have to negotiate the descent by alternating sides of the burn. Soon a clear path is encountered to the left of the burn, becoming stronger as it progresses.

The Harthope Burn runs down the length of the valley. At the bridge at Carey Burn it combines with the Carey Burn to become the Coldgate Water.

The path, now obvious, continues along the valley floor.

A picturesque spot can be found at the point where the path contours around the side of a gully. To the right is a lush grassy area with a waterfall well worth a visit – a truly delightful spot where the cares of the world seem a long way off.

Still further down the valley a loud rushing noise from the burn is heard after passing a sheep fold on your left. Leave the path and take a few steps to the right.

This is Harthope Linn, a series of pretty waterfalls fringed by ferns and trees. A sylvan hideaway.

Continue to a fence crossing the path and cross via the stile. Turn left to pass to the right of some sheep pens. At a further fence, cross by the stile. The path soon reaches a small clump of trees, fording a small stream to the cottage of Langleeford Hope.

Originally a shepherd's cottage, Langleeford Hope is now used as a holiday cottage.

The path leads behind the cottage and ascends to a gate. Pass through and continue along a stone track to the next gate.

To the left of this gate there is a signpost bearing directions to Scald Hill and Cheviot.

Go through the gate and continue, passing through further gates on your way until you reach a signpost on your left. This bears directions for Harthope Linn and Langleeford Hope.

To your right, and across the burn, is the farmstead of Langleeford, sheltered amid a group of pine trees. It was here in the autumn of 1791 that Sir Walter Scott had a pleasant holiday.

Cross the stile and join a surfaced road which leads you back to your starting point.

The Breamish Valley

The Breamish Valley, or Ingram Valley as it is also known, is the most popular in the northern Cheviots. During summer and especially at weekends and holiday periods it is a honey pot for visitors, mainly from the Tyneside and S.E. Northumberland conurbations. The valley is, initially, broad and lined with low green rolling hills but, further up, it narrows between steep-sided hills. After Peggy Bells Bridge it broadens towards Hartside farm.

The curlew symbol, set in a stone marker, shows that you are entering the Northumberland National Park. From here up to a metal bridge spanning the River Breamish, the land to your left between the road and the river provides excellent parking and picnic sites. The National Park has negotiated access to this ground with the farmer and pays him compensation for the loss of grazing. The banks of the river are lined with broom and gorse, a fragrant yellow delight in the summer.

Once across the metal bridge there is a National Park car park on the left, after which the road bends to the right with a minor turning to the left. This leads to the National Park Visitor Centre. It is well worth visiting this Centre before accessing the valley. The shop sells souvenirs and brochures about the area, also light refreshments and ices. Guided walks start from the Centre and from other points within Northumberland. A leaflet giving details is available from the information desk.

Next to the Centre is the local mountain rescue post. On the opposite side of the road from the Centre stands the Church of St Michael, some parts of which are of Norman origin. It is still used as a parish church.

Returning to the main road and continuing up the valley you pass through the picturesque village of Ingram. From here, the road continues to Bulbys Wood, where the National Park have provided a car park, toilets and picnic sites.

A kilometre further up the road brings you to Peggy Bells bridge. Peggy Bell was a young woman who drowned in the Breamish near Brandon on November 22, 1890, when the footbridge was swept away by flash floods. Beside the bridge there are parking facilities and yet more picnic and recreational sites on the fields beside the river.

From the bridge the road narrows and takes you to Hartside Farm where the public access road ends. You can, however, walk along a private road to the small hamlet of Linhope. From here, a short walk takes

Many traces of early man have been found in the Breamish Valley. The finest examples are to be found at Greaves Ash on the southern slopes of Greenshaw Hill. Covering 25 acres, it contains traces of forts, hut circles and earthworks. On Brough Law, overlooking Bulbys Wood, are the remains of a typical hill fort. Two massive ramparts encircle the top, inside which traces of hut circles can be found. Other fortified camps have been located on Knock Hill, Ewe Hill and at Reavely and Chesters. On the slopes of Heddon Hill there are ancient cultivation terraces. Ancient field systems also adorn Knock Hill, Meggrims Knowe and East Hartside.

The valley is listed as one of Britain's most important prehistoric areas. In 1995, work began on archeological excavations in parts of the valley to learn about the early population of the area. To judge by the amount of prehistoric remains, the Breamish valley must have been far more populated in the past than is the case today.

Much of the land around the Breamish Valley is owned by the Duke of Northumberland and is tenanted by individual farmers.

Walk departure points

Ingram: After crossing the metal bridge spanning the River Breamish, there is a National Park car park on the left of the road. NT018163.

Hartside: Parking is permitted on the grass verges of the road just before Hartside Farm at GR975162. Please park considerately.

14. Ingram to Chesters

A gentle climb followed by level walking, the return being downhill.

Distance: 10.5km (6.75 miles)

Grade: Easy

Maps: Ordnance Survey Landranger 81. Ordnance Survey Pathfinders 487 NT81/91 and 488 NU01/11. Ordnance Survey Outdoor Leisure 16

Start: Ingram car park. GR 018163.

Chesters Hill Fort is of ancient origin and overlooks the Breamish valley. It consists of two circular ramparts surrounding a cluster of hut circles.

On leaving the parking area turn left along the surfaced road and turn right to pass through Ingram. The road continues over a cattle grid and alongside a plantation. At the end of the plantation there is a signpost bearing directions for Chesters and Alnhammoor. Leave the road and follow a track up hill. Just before the top there is a division of the track. Take the right-hand path which continues to rise reaching a white tipped wooden marker post on level ground above. A dozen or so paces past the post turn right and follow a well-defined path which contours the side of Ewe Hill, climbing gently.

Below to your left is a derelict shepherd's cottage. This is one of many such cottages and they were usually abandoned because they did not have access to services or bus routes. As you ascend, some trees will gradually enter your line of vision on the skyline ahead. This is where you are heading.

At a white-tipped marker post the path divides. Take the left path and a dozen paces on, the path divides again. This time take the right-hand path. Walk on to the trees you saw earlier as you ascended Ewe Hill. Just before the trees there is a crossroads of paths. The correct route lies straight ahead towards a gate in the wire fence next to the plantation.

The trees are enclosed within a large square stone wall. They mostly consist of ash, elder and beech with an occasional Scots pine. You may occasionally see a huge rabbit-like creature hereabouts. It is not a big rabbit but a hare. Hares live above ground and have longer ears and legs and do not possess a white tail. They run rather than hop and when disturbed usually zig-zag across the open ground to avoid capture.

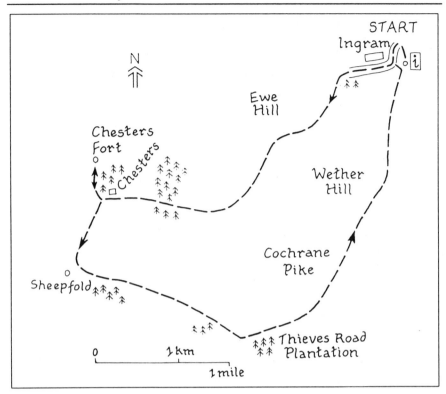

Cross the fence using the stile next to the gate and continue across a field to another gate set in a wire fence, visible on the skyline ahead. Cross via the stile. The path travels half-left. When you reach the point where the path forks take the lesser path leading off to the right, curving around the slope of a hill. 'Chesters' is to the right.

Originally a farm house, it was later abandoned. In 1968, Whitley Bay Boy Scouts adopted it as an outdoor activities centre.

The path drops to a plantation set in a bowl shaped depression. A small gate allows you to enter the trees. After fording a small burn the path ascends through coniferous trees alongside a small burn to another gate allowing you to leave the plantation. Chesters is ahead. Walk towards it until you encounter a stone wall with a wire fence. Turn left here and follow the wall to reach a gate. Go through and along a path which takes you behind Chesters to another gate. Pass through this and join a red-stone track. Walk on for some 30 metres to a marker post. Turn right here and cross a grassy area to the site of Chesters hill fort.

The fort is sited in a position which allowed it to command an impressive view over the surrounding land. Ramparts and traces of hut circles are clearly visible.

Return to the marker post and turn right to follow the stone track up a slight rise to a wire fence. Go through the gate and walk on until, just before a plantation, the track bends to the right. At this point leave the track and continue straight ahead over a grass path to a fence running across the path from a plantation to your right.

You may well hear a loud 'curlee cur-lee' as you cross this stretch. This is the haunting cry of the curlew – the bird with the long curving beak which is the symbol of the Northumberland National Park. Its lone cry typifies this land of wide open spaces.

Pass through the gate and along a track parallel to the plantation. At the end of the plantation the track continues descending towards a burn before climbing up a hill side. At the top of the hill the path encounters a stone wall, with a plantation to the right. Pass through the gate in the wall.

Ahead and below there is a panoramic view of the surrounding countryside and the Vale of Whittingham. On the skyline are the outlines of the Simonside Hills above Rothbury. The small hamlet seen below is that of Prendwick.

There are several paths from the gate. The correct one turns half-left and follows a broad track which curves around a slope to pass above a mixed plantation underplanted with rhododendrons.

Rhododendrons are not native to this country. They were introduced during Victorian times and originated from the Himalayas. A large collection of rhododendrons can be viewed at the Hirsel Country Park, near Coldstream, seat of the late Sir Alec Douglas Home.

Continue through a gate and along the top of a coniferous plantation which adjoins it. The path passes this plantation before crossing open ground to a wire fence. Turn right here and through a gate. At this point, leave the path and descend over grass to a further gate in the fence to your left. Cross over the stile and continue contouring Cochrane Pike. At a fence, cross via the stile.

As the way ascends, the view to the east over Northumberland expands.

The path contours Wether Hill and begins descending towards Ingram. Pass through a gate and remain on the path to pass through further gates to a final gate leading on to a surfaced road. Turn right and follow the road as it bends left to the National Park Information Centre. To the left of the car parking area a well-marked footpath leads through trees to return you to your starting point.

15. Hartside to High Cantle

An adventurous walk for those completing the whole circuit.

Distance: 12.8km (8 miles)

Grade: see above

Maps: Ordnance Survey Landrangers 80 & 81. Ordnance Survey Pathfinder 487 NT81/91. Ordnance Survey Outdoor Leisure 16

Start: At GR975162 next to Hartside Farm

The first part of the walk, the section to Bleakhope is easy, but the later stages can be difficult over lengthy stretches of indistinct or nonexistent paths. It is strongly advised this last section should not be attempted in bad visibility or deep snow. The rough hillocks and wet moorland leading to Rig Cairn may easily cause sprained ankles or worse. An escape route is available from Low Bleakhope, avoiding the traverse of High Cantle.

Take the private road signposted for Alnhammoor to a bridge spanning Linhope Burn. Cross over and ascend to a marker post just before the farm. Turn left off the road to reach a fence. Cross via the stile and over a small paddock to a gate in a stone wall. Pass through and turn right along a farm track. Where the track bends right, continue straight ahead to a wire fence. Cross using the ladder stile. The path then drops into a valley to cross a plank bridge over a narrow burn. Continue along the path guided by marker posts, soon rising out of the valley.

Shank Burn, which is on your left, later flows into the River Breamish. Beside these upland burns a popular bird is the dipper, easily identified by its white breast and short tail. It may be seen sitting on stones beside the burn frequently bobbing up and down. Its startling habit is to 'fly' into the water, wings outstretched, often emerging with a small fish or water beetle.

Continue across a stretch of rough grass before climbing up the slope of Scaud Knowe. Before the top the path bends left and contours around the upper slopes of the hill, marker posts guiding you along. The path descends slightly to a crossroads of paths with a marker post set in a small cairn. Turn right here, as indicated by a blue arrow, then ascend a good rising path.

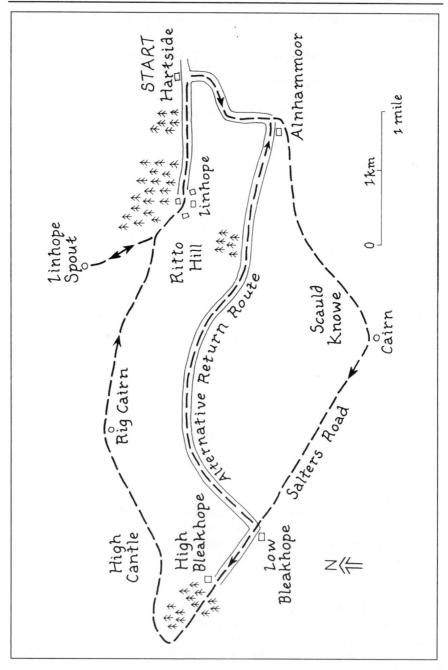

You are now on Salters Road. In olden times when meat could only be preserved by salting or smoking, salt was a valuable commodity. This route was used by traders transporting salt from the English coastal salt pans at Alnmouth to Scotland. For these reasons the way became known as the Salters Road. Before this, in the fourteenth century, it was known as 'Theeves Rode' frequently used by thieves and smugglers. The salt carriers were not averse to carrying flagons, known as grey hens, of illicit whisky along with their legitimate stock in trade.

On the plateau, continue until the path descends to a wire fence. Pass through the gate and on to a track over heather-clad ground, traversing level ground for 200 metres before making the descent towards Low Bleakhope farm.

As you approach the end of the plateau a stunning view opens up ahead as the upper Breamish Valley appears, the ground dropping away in front of you. The view below and ahead is stupendous.

The track descends the right-hand side of the valley, later joining a good farm track which takes you down to the valley floor. Just before the bungalow at Low Bleakhope a small burn has to be forded. The track runs to the right of the bungalow to join a surfaced road.

From this point, you can return to the start by turning right and following the road which returns you to Alnhammoor. Those more experienced and properly attired may continue. Boots, maps and compass, and the ability to use them are all advisable when crossing High Cantle in adverse conditions. Boots are definitely needed.

If continuing, turn left along the road with the River Breamish on your right and the steep side of Low Cantle. Walk on for a kilometre, turn right and cross the bridge spanning the river. Once over the bridge turn left to follow the road to High Bleakhope. Pass through the farm buildings, via gates, to a small plantation. A gate allows entry and a short walk takes you through the trees to another gate, where you exit. Continue on a stone track until you reach a further gate. Go through and walk on to pass to the left of a small stand of ancient alder trees and reach a gate set in a stone wall.

This is an excellent spot to stop for a refreshment break before the ascent of High Cantle. The route ahead climbs steeply from 330m to 482m in the space of a half kilometre.

After pausing, go through the gate and along the track to a wooden marker post just before a wire fence. Turn right here and follow the path as it begins the ascent of High Cantle. At a wire fence go through the gate and continue climbing as the path leads ever upwards, marker posts guiding you along. Eventually you will reach a wire fence at the top, I promise you. Pass through the gate and turn half-right to climb a small hillock to (currently) a dilapidated rusty wire fence. Cross over and turn half-left over rough heather-covered ground to the small cairn (not yet visible) of Rig Cairn ahead.

The above section involves crossing a kilometre of rough ground with no marker posts or distinctive paths to help. It is a case of making your way as best you can. The best guide is to aim for the two low mounds ahead below the distinctive rocky summit of Great Staindrop easily seen on the skyline. On nearing the mounds, the cairn on Rig Cairn is seen on the top of the right-hand mound. This path is particularly dangerous in snowy weather when hazards such as deep holes can not be seen.

From Rig Cairn, follow the track to the left of the cairn as it descends towards Linhope. Pass through a gate and continue on the track as it bends to the left of Ritto Hill heading towards a plantation. The path soon joins a forestry road where you turn right.

At this point there is a signpost bearing directions to Linhope Spout. This is an impressive waterfall and well worth the diversion if time and energy permit.

Continue along the forest road and through a gate in a stone wall. The track then turns left towards Linhope. Pass through the hamlet and continue up and along the surfaced road to return to your starting point.

16. Hartside to Salters Road

A walk along part of a historic trading and smuggling route

Distance: 11.3km (7 miles)

Grade: Moderate

Maps: Ordnance Survey Landranger 81. Ordnance Survey Pathfinder 487 NT81/91. Ordnance Survey Outdoor Leisure 16

Start: At GR975162 next to Hartside Farm

Salters Road is an old trade route between England and Scotland. It dates back from prehistoric times. The name is derived from the salt traders who used this route in medieval times. The salt was obtained from the coastal salt pans in England and taken by pack horse to Scotland. Much of it was smuggled to avoid payment of tax. The road was also used by Border Reivers, drovers and thieves. It was also used for whisky smuggling, the whisky being carried in flagons known as 'grey hens'.

Take the road leading to your left, signposted for Alnhammoor. Cross the bridge spanning the Shank Burn and ascend towards the buildings of Alnhammoor farm. Just before the farm, a marker post with a yellow arrow directs you to the left. Turn as directed, leaving the road and after a few paces come to a fence Cross the stile and head over a small paddock to exit by a gate in a stone wall ahead. Now turn left and descend to a metal gate. Pass through and cross the burn via a wooden foot bridge.

The Shank Burn flows into the River Breamish a little to the southeast of Alnhammoor.

Follow the track to a metal gate and use the stile to cross over. Go half-right over a grassy path towards a gate in the top right-hand corner of the field. Pass through the gate and follow a broad track which rises gently. A wire fence is to your left.

This track can be muddy after a spell of wet weather.

Later, the fence turns sharply left away from the track, which continues to rise. At the top corner of a plantation the track dips steeply to ford a burn before rising to a gate.

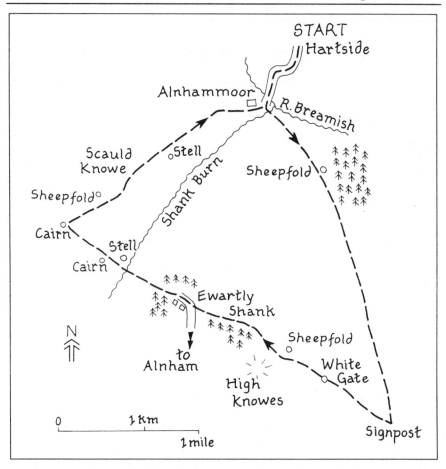

Pause on the ascent to look back. You can see Alnhammoor below with Staindrop to the right and, to the left, the dome of Hedgehope. To the left and behind Hedgehope looms the great massif that is Cheviot.

Cross the stile and walk along a grassy track. When you reach a fork in the track, take the less distinct path leading off right and ascend to a gate. Pass through and continue along the track to eventually join up with a red stone track. Continue along till you reach a marker post. Turn sharp right and follow a grass track, this is Salters Road. Follow the track to ford a small burn and then reach a stone wall with a gate. Cross via the stile to the side of the gate.

On maps, this point is marked as 'White gate', but currently is a metal gate painted blue! If you choose to rest by a stone wall take note of any small burrows or entrances in the wall face as they could conceal an

Salters Road

adder or a weasel, either of which may inflict a nasty bite if disturbed or frightened. Though adders are venomous their bite is generally non-fatal. However, if bitten, keep calm and seek medical help quickly. An anti-histamine will normally be prescribed. Dogs are more susceptible, and may die of an adder bite.

There are marker arrows on the gate, our route takes us to the right. About a half kilometre on the path passes to the left of a stone sheep fold. It then contours around the side of High Knowes. At a fork in the track take the right hand turning which will take you to a wire fence. Pass through the gate and follow the path as it leads you to a plantation and along the side of it. Pass through the gate and make the slight descent to the farm road. Turn right and follow the road to Ewartly Shank.

On 19th century and earlier maps, the farm is marked as Elsdon Shank. On the summit of High Knowes are the remains of a palisaded settlement dating from about 1800 BC, but it is not easily discernible. It would have consisted of a cluster of circular wooden huts surrounded by a wooden stockade.

Pass in front of the bungalow then left to a wooden gate. Pass through the gate and turn right to a stile crossing the fence to your right. Cross the stile and then turn left to a gate leading into a plantation. Pass through the trees to another gate which allows you to exit from the trees. Descend into a valley via a path leading to a ford across the burn. Head towards a gate in the fence above climbing out of the valley and ascend towards the top of Little Dod.

Some way up, there is a cairn to the left of the path which should not be mistaken for the summit, as there is still a little way to go. The summit itself is quite flat and has no cairn (as yet).

Cross the summit and descend to a small cairn of stones around a marker post. Turn right here, as indicated by a yellow arrow. The path contours around the slope of Scaud Knowe and is clearly marked by wooden marker posts with yellow arrows.

There are some fine views from this path, including Cheviot, the Northumbrian coastal plain and, to the right, the Simonside Hills etched against the skyline. Behind Little Dod rises Hogden Law, with its distinctive summit cairn.

Soon the farm of Alnhammoor appears ahead, the path descending to a wire fence. Go through the gate and along a path which gradually veers right and down into a shallow valley. Continue to a plank bridge spanning a narrow burn. Cross and climb the path ahead, ignoring a tractor track leading off to the left. The path rises to a wire fence crossed via a ladder stile. A grass path leads behind the farm buildings to a stone wall. A few paces on, pass through a gate in the wall and cross a small paddock to a stile. Climb over and on to a surfaced road. Turn right and follow it to return to your starting point.

17. Hartside to Linhope Spout

A pleasant non-strenuous walk, suitable for families. Try to avoid high days and holidays when planning this walk as the path can resemble a bus queue on sunny Bank Holidays.

Distance: 7.2km (4.5 miles)

Grade: Easy

Maps: Ordnance Survey Landranger 75. Ordnance Survey Pathfinder 487 NT81/91. Ordnance Survey Outdoor Leisure 16

Start: At GR975162 next to Hartside Farm

Linhope Spout is one of the finest waterfalls in the northern Cheviots. It has a drop of 17 metres into a rocky basin. As with all waterfalls it is best seen at its best after a period of wet weather. This idyllic spot offers an excellent picnic site which can prove very popular.

Take the surfaced road leading past Hartside farm to a gate, here a notice states 'Private road-no vehicles'. Pass through the gate and continue along the surfaced road leading you to the tiny hamlet of Linhope. To your right, across the fields, are the stark slopes of Dunmoor Hill.

The first plantation you pass on your right is underplanted with rhododendron bushes to provide cover for game birds. Behind the next plantation, also on your right, lies the settlement of Greaves Ash, dating back from Romano-British times. The main settlement consisted of thirty stone-built roundhouses. A smaller settlement of ten houses has been found 250 metres to the north-east. The remains of a double walled Iron Age fort can also be found on the eastern shoulder of the hill. To visit the site, pass through the iron gate at the start of the plantation, walk on a few paces to a wooden gate, go through and turn left to ascend the hill.

Cross over the stone-built bridge and enter Linhope. Keep on the road and follow as it bends sharply left to a gate at the end of the road. This is signposted for Linhope Spout. Pass through the gate and follow the track as it takes a loop to the right to a gate set in a stone wall. Pass through this gate, and Linhope Wood is on your right.

Linhope Wood is private property and walkers are asked to refrain from

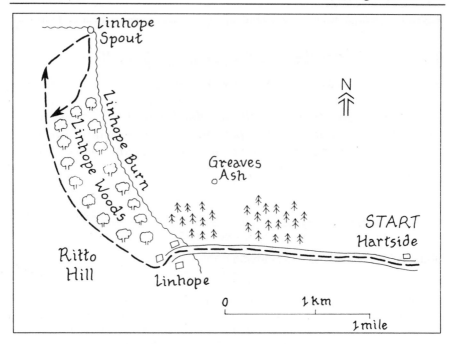

entering. The wood contains a variety of trees and is underplanted with rhododendrons. Small waterfalls can be heard along the burn below hidden by the trees.

The track gently climbs around the west side of Linhope Wood. After three hundred metres the main track travels away from the wood. At this point take the lesser path leading off to the right. It is signposted for Linhope Spout. Continue along the track adjoining the wood to a gate.

The main track veers away to grouse moors.

Go through the gate on to rough pasture and follow the grass path for some 360 metres to the top of Linhope Spout. Descend, with care, to the base using the rocky path to the left of the falls.

Take time now to have a refreshment break and enjoy the beauty of the falls. Yellow wagtails frequent this burn. This small bird usually breeds beside fresh water streams. The male of the species is the most brilliantly coloured yellow of all British birds. Wagtails are known for their habit of wagging their tails up and down – not surprisingly. The yellow wagtail is a summer visitor.

Reluctantly, it is time to return. Turn right, away from the falls, and along a good grass path by the side of the tumbling Linhope Burn. The path begins to climb a steep rise out of the valley. At the top turn right and along the side of Linhope Wood to the main track.

Many birds are present in these woods to your left including blackbirds, song thrush, tits, wrens and pheasant. The track seems to have more than its fair share of rabbits.

Go through the gate on your left and follow the track to Linhope. From here, follow the surfaced road to return to Hartside and the start of your walk.

As you pass the plantations to your left you may spot some roe deer. These are small creatures, reddish brown in colour, with a white patch under their tail known as the target. They average 65cm in height.

Linhope Spout

The Bowmont Valley

This valley is wide and open, running deep into the heart of the Cheviot range. Lined with undulating green hills, it is one of the most serene and scenic of the Scottish valleys in the northern Cheviots. Meandering down its centre the Bowmont Water flows pure and fresh, the haunt of darting brown trout, dippers and heron.

Bowmont valley has witnessed man's struggle for survival since pre-history. There are many settlements, hut circles and cultivation terraces within its bounds. Later the monks of Melrose farmed the valley and traces of their occupation are also present. Sourhope, with its experimental agricultural station, is conducting new and exciting experiments in upland management continuing the valley's agricultural heritage.

Beginning at Primeside Farm, a narrow surfaced road leads you through the valley. Arable land and rough pasture line the road, while side tracks lead off to the various farms in the valley.

Some 6.5km down the road lies Belford Farm. Looking left across the Bowmont Water you can imagine prehistoric man in the cultivation terraces on the slopes of Mow Law. Below the terraces are traces of a settlement, probably of the same period.

A further 1.6km down the road, you pass a private camping site – very basic but containing a toilet block. The road then continues to curve around the middle slopes of Mow Law to a fork.

The left fork travels just under 0.5km to Sourhope. Here, there is an experimental agricultural station and a farm. It is utilised by the Scottish agricultural colleges to give work experience to students on a hill farm setting.

Taking the right fork, the road dips to cross the Bowmont Water and continues for 2km to the large farm at Cocklawfoot. At this point the valley splits. The valley leading off to the left follows the course of the Cheviot Burn up to the Border ridge. A farm track leads you through the second valley to the right to the farm at Kelsocleugh. From here the valley continues for about 1km to end in a large basin beneath the Border ridge. The Kelsocleugh Burn running down the valley to Cocklawfoot has its birth on the slopes of Windy Gyle.

From Cocklawfoot, an old drovers' road known as Clennell Street rises to the Border ridge before descending into the Coquet Valley, finally ending at Alwinton.

Wildlife abounds within the valley. At the right time, preferably early morning or dusk, you may catch sight of roe deer, fox, badger and heron. You may also see kestrel, sparrow hawk and occasionally a merlin. There are short-eared and barn owls to be seen.

Walk departure points

Belford: There is parking space on the grass verge of the road opposite the telephone box at Belford GR815208.

Cocklawfoot: On the grass verges of the road just before the bridge spanning the Kelsocleugh Burn and leading into Cocklawfoot Farm GR852186.

18. Belford to Hownam Rings

A good walk, steeped in history

Distance: 14.4km (9 miles)

Grade: Easy

Maps: Ordnance Survey Landranger 80. Ordnance Survey Pathfinder 487 NT81/91 and 475 NT82/92 and 486 NT61/71. Ordnance Survey Outdoor Leisure 16

Start: At GR815208 opposite the telephone box at Belford

Hownam Rings is the site of a prehistoric walled settlement. It covers an area of 22 acres and traces of up to 155 houses have been discovered. The first settlement here was protected by a single palisade. This was later replaced by a stone wall about 3 metres (10 feet) thick. Later still three ramparts were added. With the arrival of the Romans the defences were removed and an open settlement spread out over the area possibly due to the 'Pax Romana'.

Take the stone track to the right of the public telephone box to pass to the left of a cottage. Keep to the track as it gently climbs Belford Hope. Pass through gates to the top of the saddle between Wondrum Hill on your left and The Kip on your right. The track continues descending through gates to a stone wall with a gate at the bottom of the slope.

On the descent from the saddle you will notice a ruin to your right, this was the shepherd's cottage of Seefew. With the advent of the car and the modern way of life, few shepherds wished to live in these cottages with little or no mains services and far from shops and schools.

After passing through the gate, the path makes a brief descent to cross the Hownam Burn before climbing in a curve to another burn which is easily forded. The path continues to ascend Windy Law. On arriving at the top the path heads towards a gate set in a stone wall. Just before the gate another broad path crosses your path. At this point turn right on to this path and follow it to Hownam Rings hill fort and settlement.

The path is 'The Street', an old drovers' road running from Hownam to Alwinton. Its age is unknown though possibly dating from pre-Roman times. On approaching the site a line of standing stones crosses the path. These are the 'Shearers', their purpose unknown. According to legend

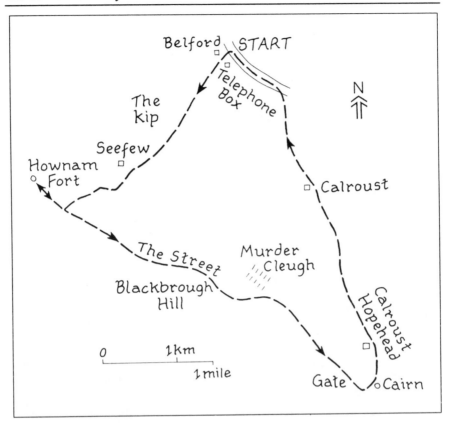

the Shearers were originally eleven people who had been working in the field shearing corn on the Sabbath Day. As a punishment for working on this holy day they were transformed into blocks of stone and remain to this day as a remainder to others. Take note if you are walking on this hill on a Sunday.

After exploring the site at your leisure, return to the Street, keeping the stone wall on your right. Continue along this pleasant green track southwards.

Dry-stone walls were generally built around here between 1850-1890 and have a life expectancy of two hundred years.

Later, the track descends steeply and the stone wall is replaced by a wire fence. At this point there is a gate in the fence. Pass through and turn left to ford a small burn and follow the track as it climbs to Craik Moor. Keep the wire fence on the left.

The valley to the right leads to Greenhill farm via a narrow path.

Later you reach a gate in a fence crossing your way. There is a fence leading off to your right and if you follow alongside this fence, you will reach the hill fort on Blackbrough Hill. There is no clear path leading to the fort but the fence is sufficient guide.

Blackbrough Hill Iron Age fortification has a rampart around it some 100 metres in circumference. Traces of hut circles can be discerned on the ground. From the fort there is a commanding view of the Heather-hope Valley.

Return to the track by retracing your steps. Descend to a gate. Pass through this and then another a few steps on. The path now climbs a slope.

Looking down the valley on your left one can see the farmhouse of Calroust. This is a handy escape route if the weather closes in. Over-looking it to the right is Murder Cleugh. How it gained this name is a mystery, perhaps some foul deed on an unwary traveller in the past may have contributed to its christening.

Continue along the track with a wire fence to your right, passing through gates along the way. Further on, cross a watershed tributary to the Calroust Burn. Walk on till you reach a gate set in the fence on your right. The gate leads into the Heatherhope Valley.

Pass by the gate. The track climbs a small rise. Watch carefully for a cairn on the hill crest to your left. On sighting it leave the track and head over heather towards it. Just before the cairn you will come upon a tractor track. Turn left on to it and continue as it travels to the left of the cairn and down to the floor of the valley.

There are some excellent views of the valley as you descend while, to your right, Cheviot looms as a mighty bulk on the skyline.

At the foot of the track, ford a burn and pass on to a farm track to continue through a gate in a stone wall across the track. The derelict farmhouse of Calroust, surrounded by a stand of old trees, is passed on your left.

The farm house is not lived in, but local shepherds sometimes use it during lambing time. The empty shed to the right of the house provides a fine shelter if you are caught out in a sudden downpour.

Continue to a stone wall across the track and a gate.

Just before the gate, look to your left for the unusual sight of two intertwined trees. Comprising of an alder and a mountain ash, they give the appearance of springing from one trunk. The mountain ash, or rowan as it is more commonly known, is usually sown in rocky clefts or tree trunks after passing unharmed through the digestive system of birds. The rowan has long been associated with witchcraft. Among other uses, its wood was used in ceremonial fires during fertility rites. Another claim for this magical tree was that chewing a piece of bark protected one from witches when out at night. Furthermore a twig could be used to ward off evil spirits. Cutting a branch on Ascension day and hanging it over your door was said to protect the house and its occupants from the Devil and his work.

The clear track continues along the valley. Below to your right flows the Calroust Burn, fringed by alder trees.

Alder trees are very hardy but prefer damp soil near water.

Eventually you will arrive at Calroust farm.

The hills above and to the right exhibit many signs of ancient civilisations. It was while walking down the track with my wife and daughter that we witnessed the exciting sight of two foxes cavorting on the hillside. Playing and jumping, their jubilant barks delighted our ears, before they scampered off over the skyline and became lost to sight.

At the farm, do not go through the first gate in the stone wall to your left, but continue for a few paces to a second gate. This leads to another gate and on to a surfaced road. This takes you through the farm. Continue on this road to join up with the Cocklawfoot road. At this point observe the Monkey Puzzle tree to your left. These trees are surprisingly hardy and were planted for ornamental value. Turn left along the road to return to your starting point.

The ruins of Seefew

19. Cocklawfoot to the Schil

An energetic walk, but worth it on completion – a chance to stretch your legs.

Distance: 12.5km (8 miles)

Grade: Moderate

Maps: Ordnance Survey Landranger 80 and 74. Ordnance Survey Pathfinders 487 NT81/91 and 475 NT82/92. Ordnance Survey Outdoor Leisure 16.

Start: At GR852186 before the bridge into Cocklawfoot Farm

Situated north-west of Cheviot, the Schill is the third highest summit of the range. At 613 metres (1985 feet) it provides a fine viewpoint over looking Scotland and England.

Leave the parking area and cross the bridge spanning Kelsocleugh Burn. Walk along the farm track and through Cocklawfoot farm. Go through a gate and continue to a bridge spanning the burn to your left. Cross the bridge and follow a path as it climbs towards a small hill. At the base of this hill the path turns half-right and leads to a gate in a wire fence. Go through and turn sharp left to pass through another gate. Turn right now and begin the ascent of Auchope Rig with a fence to your right. At a wire fence at the top go through the gates there and forward a few paces to the well-trodden path of the Pennine Way.

Looking to your right, you will see the square shape of the mountain rescue hut. Behind it is Hen Hole with Cheviot looming to the left of it.

Turn left along the Way and, keeping a fence on your left, follow an eroded peaty track to the top of the Schil. The summit cairn is located on the other side of the fence. This is best reached by crossing the fence at the point where it bends left and walking straight ahead to the impressive rocky top. Return to the fence and cross over. Turn left and continue to follow the path of the Pennine Way as it descends from the summit. Pass to the left of some rocky outcrops and continue to a wire fence across the path. Cross via the stile. By now the wire fence to your left has been replaced by stone wall. Continue beside this wall to a ladder stile.

There is a signpost here bearing directions for Pennine Way, Kirk Yetholm and Mounthooly.

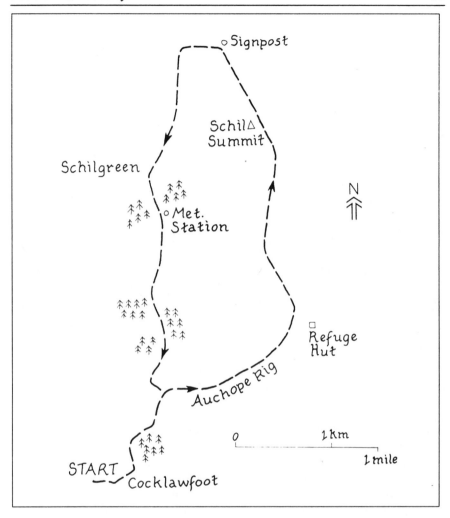

Cross over the wall using the ladder stile and continue straight ahead on a grass path for about 200 metres to a marker post. Turn left here on to a grass path which leads into the valley on your left. The path leads around the lower slopes of the Schil before dropping to a fence with a gate, which you pass through.

The elongated hump of The Curr is to your right.

At the base of the valley, pass through a gate with a cattle grid and turn left along a forestry road which rises to another gate.

The view to the east from the summit

A meteorological station is located to the left of this gate.

Pass over the cattle grid and continue along the track to a metal gate. Pass through and turn left to go along the side of a plantation. Go through another gate and on to where the path bends gently to the right. Turn left through yet another gate here turn left, leaving the track, and climb the steep rise keeping a wire fence to your right. From the top, pass through two wooden gates, ignoring a metal one.

Coniferous plantations in the Cheviots include four species of tree: Sitka Spruce; Norway Spruce; Scots Pine and Larch. All are ideally suited to the area as they establish themselves easily in peaty soil and survive the often harsh conditions.

Follow a grassy path leading slightly left to contour around the base of a low hill. Ahead lies a plantation and the path leads to the top left corner. Just before it a fence crosses the path. Go through the gate in the fence and along the top edge of the plantation. When the trees end, continue and keep a wire fence on your left, until you reach a gate in the fence. Pass through and descend rough ground to a wooden bridge spanning the Cheviot Burn. Cross over and turn right on to a farm road which will return you to Cocklawfoot and your starting point.

20. Cocklawfoot to Windy Gyle

A steady climb up to Windy Gyle, excellent views, good clear paths.

Distance: 9.6km (6 miles)

Grade: Strenuous

Maps: Ordnance Survey Landranger 80. Ordnance Survey Pathfinder 487 NT81/91. Ordnance Survey Outdoor Leisure 16

Start: At GR852186 next to bridge leading into Cocklawfoot Farm

The summit of Windy Gyle is marked by a large cairn surmounted with an Ordnance Survey column. Originally a bronze age burial mound, Russell's Cairn was named in memory of Lord Francis Russell, who was killed during a March Wardens meeting at nearby Hexpethgate in 1558.

Climb to the right of the parking area, then continue left on a good farm track to pass through a gate. Continue along the track to another gate leading into Kelsocleugh farm. Turn right at the gate and follow a grass path next to the stone wall to a ladder stile. Cross over the wall.

The plantations in the area are mainly coniferous. In 1919, after depletion of the timber supply during the First World War, the Forestry Commission was set up to replenish the forests and ensure a good reserve of timber for future needs. The trees are felled when they reach maturity after 40 to 50 years.

Go diagonally across two rough pasture fields towards the gap in the plantation ahead. The path climbs through the trees to emerge on open ground at the top. Turn right and through a gate. The path bends right, rising gently, and parallel to a wire fence to your right. Where the fence turns right, leave it and bear half-left, contouring the aptly-named Windy Rig above the bowl-shaped depression of the valley to your left.

The view now opens up dramatically with Cheviot behind you and the full stretch of the Border Ridge to your left. As you continue climbing the view to the right into Scotland opens up with seemingly endless hills.

Cross a stretch of open ground to join a wire fence coming in from the right. The path then curves to the left. Pass through the gate there and follow a

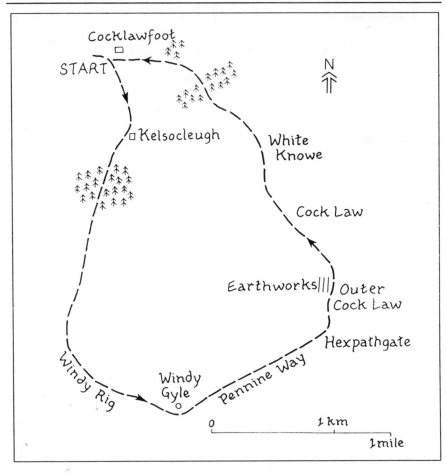

well-trodden path (the Pennine Way) to ascend Windy Gyle. Continue to a stile to recross the fence. After a short climb, a track leading off to the left takes you to the summit of Windy Gyle which is topped with an Ordnance Survey column.

The first Ordnance Survey was carried out in 1791. At the time, the south-east coast was under threat of a possible invasion from France and proper maps were needed by the British army. The first mappings were carried out by the Board of Ordnance, an army department responsible for engineering and ammunition. The first map was published in 1801. With the coming of the Industrial revolution, accurate maps were needed to develop new roads and towns, so the Ordnance Survey mapping was extended to cover the whole country. The first

Looking north from the Border ridge

maps were to a scale of one inch to one mile and later maps at larger scales were produced for greater accuracy. Now a civilian government department, the Ordnance Survey produces maps by automated carto-graphic technology from computer data banks that are updated from satellite data. A far cry from those early days when men using chains and tapes measured the country on foot.

Walk south from the cairn to a gate in a wire fence. Go through and turn left to follow the well-trodden path of the Pennine Way. At a fence, pass through the gate.

To combat erosion of the peat, stone slabs have been laid along sections of the walk. A welcome relief after peat bog hopping.

Continue for about 2km to a gate in the fence with a four-finger signpost to the right of it.

This is Hexpethgate. In the 15th and 16th centuries, when Border warfare was at its peak, this was a neutral meeting place for the Lords Wardens of the Marches to hold talks and attempt to sort out local disputes. It was here in 1558 that Lord Francis Russell, accompanying his father-in-law, Sir John Forster of Bamburgh Castle, was fatally shot during one of these meetings.

Go through the gate to descend a broad well-defined track following the route to Cocklawfoot as shown by the signpost. The track curves around the slope of Outer Cock Law to a gate in a wire fence.

The middle slopes of Outer Cock Law bear traces of ancient earthworks, visible today as a series of ridges above to your left.

Pass through the gate and cross the broad top of Cock Law. Later the track descends in a large curve to contour the side of White Knowe. Below and to your left is the farm of Kelsocleugh and your outward route. The track leads through a gap in a small plantation.

Many traces of forts and homesteads adorn the hillside. The track you are walking on is an old drovers' road called Clennell Street. It was used in medieval times by drovers herding their livestock between Cocklaw-foot and Alwinton in Coquetdale.

Pass through the gate exiting from the plantation and make the final descent on a rough tractor track to Cocklawfoot. Go through the gate in the stone wall and turn left to cross the wooden bridge spanning the Kelsocleugh Burn and arrive back at your starting point.

21. Cocklawfoot to Auchope

*A climb to the Border Ridge, along part of the Pennine Way and
back down the lonely Cheviot Burn.*

Distance: 13km (8 miles)

Grade: Strenuous

Maps: Ordnance Survey Landranger 80 and 74. Ordnance Survey Pathfinder 487 NT81/91. Ordnance Survey Outdoor Leisure 16

Start: GR852186, next to Cocklawfoot Farm.

Auchope Cairn, standing at 737 metres (2418 feet) is an excellent viewpoint providing extensive views deep into Scotland. It is claimed that on clear days, using binoculars, it is possible to see the shape of Lochnagar, near Balmoral 100km away.

Cross the wooden bridge leading into Cocklawfoot farm. Before reaching the house, pass through a gate in the stone wall to your right beside a large sycamore tree. Climb the broad track leading to a gap in the plantation ahead which you enter by a gate.

This is Clennell Street, an ancient trading route believed to be pre-Roman. It stretches a distance of 19km from Alwinton in England to Hownam in Scotland. In medieval times it was a popular route for the smuggling of whisky.

A short walk takes you through the conifers, from where the track climbs in a large curve around the upper slope of White Law to the summit of Cock Law. Cross its broad top and follow the track as it makes a slight descent to a gate in a wire fence. Pass through the gate and continue on the track.

Ancient earthworks, as ridges, can be seen above and to the right as you ascend Outer Cock Law. The word 'law' is derived from the old English 'hlaw' meaning a hill.

Continue on a grassy track to a wire fence at the top with a gate. There is a four-finger signpost on the other side.

This is Hexpethgate, used in bygone days as a Border crossing point. Here, you leave the ancient route of Clennal Street and join the Pennine Way.

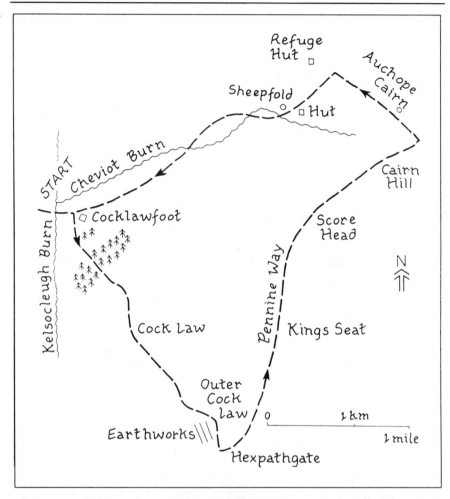

Go through the gate and turn left to follow the well-trodden path of the Pennine Way along the Border ridge and across the broad tops of King's Seat and Score Head.

This section of the walk suffers badly from erosion. Keep the wire fence within sight at all times. It is your guide, companion and lifeline if mist or cloud descend to blanket the area. Stretches of mill-stones have been laid at intervals to inhibit further damage to the path.

After crossing Score Head the path veers half-right to begin the ascent of Cairn Hill. Keep to the path until you reach a point where the fence bends left and you reach a stile with a Pennine Way signpost.

Looking to Scotland from Auchope cairn

Wooden duckboards have been laid towards the end of this stretch leading to the stile, again to combat erosion. This length of path was installed by the National Park Voluntary Warden Service during July/August 1981. A signpost here bears directions for the Pennine Way and Cheviot summit.

Cross over the stile and continue over duckboards to the impressive stone cairns on Auchope Cairn. After Auchope the path descends steeply until you reach a point where the path levels out before climbing again. There is a gate in the fence to your left. Pass through the gate and walk straight ahead over rough ground covered in coarse grass. Make your descent to the valley floor on this indistinct path. This is obscured in snowy weather. On reaching the valley floor and the Cheviot Burn, turn right and pass to the right of an old railway waggon then, after a few steps, to the left of a stone sheep fold. Continue along the track as it meanders down the valley.

To your right rises the steep flank of Auchope Rig. Sheep folds were built with stone walls and were used to gather sheep in for feeding or lambing.

At first the path zigzags back and forth, often forcing you to ford the burn. The track eventually settles for the left-hand side of the burn. Further down the valley the track rises and later reaches a slope above a derelict wooden bridge to your right. Climb the slope keeping a wire fence to your right to a gate in the fence, pass through.

The bridge had been swept away by flooding of the valley in 1995. Hopefully, it will have been rebuilt by the time you are reading this book.

Once through the gate, descend a gentle slope to pass between a corrugated metal shed and a stone sheep fold. Continue to the bank of the Cheviot Burn. Turn left and make your way across the ground above the burn to a broad tractor track. Turning left follow this track to Cocklawfoot Farm. Pass quietly through the buildings and over the bridge spanning the Kelsocleugh Burn to return to your starting point.

The Heatherhope Valley

Of the five valleys covered in this section of the book, the Heatherhope Valley is surely the most remote and lonely. Beginning at Greenhill farm and surrounded by high grassy hills, the valley runs for 5km before reaching the Border ridge.

From Greenhill farm, a tarmac private road leads through the valley for 1.5km to Heatherhope Farm. A rough track then leads past the dark still waters of the now redundant Heatherhope reservoir and continues to the base of Phillip Shank. From here, a short steep climb brings you to the Border ridge.

Heatherhope reservoir once supplied the people of Kelso and surrounding areas with all their water needs, but is now no longer used.

About 1km along the valley from Greenhill lies Blackbrough Hill. Its summit is crowned with the remains of a prehistoric hill fort. From its lofty ramparts there is a commanding view of the valley. Next to it, on Greenbrough Hill the traces of an old all timber homestead within a rectangular enclosure have been found.

Walk departure point

Greenhill: roadside at GR 788175. Please park considerately on the grass verges alongside the road leading to the farm at Greenhill.

22. Heatherhope Valley Circular

A circular walk encompassing the Heatherhope Valley. One stiff climb at the end of the valley and easy level walking back via 'The Street'.

Distance: 10.3km (6.5 miles)

Grade: Moderate

Maps: Ordnance Survey Landranger 80. Ordnance Survey Pathfinders 486 NT61/71 and 487 NT81/91. Ordnance Survey Outdoor Leisure 16

Start: At GR788175 roadside before Greenhill Farm

Take the road leading off to the left of the farm and pass through a gate bearing a 'No Dogs' sign. Continue along a surfaced road as it leads up the Heatherhope Valley. After 1.6km you reach a gated wire fence crossing the road. Go through the gate. The road descends to pass to the left of Heatherhope farm and then leads up to the dam before Heatherhope reservoir. A stone track leads up and to the right, alongside the reservoir.

The reservoir is now redundant. Originally, it supplied the town of Kelso with its water supply under the auspices of the Kelso Water Works.

The track continues past the reservoir and after a few dozen steps fords a small burn before passing a farm shelter. The track fords a second burn before climbing up the steep slope of Phillip Shank.

Pause as you ascend to look back and admire the fine view of the valley and the reservoir, enclosed by Scottish hills rolling off into the distance. It also allows you a breather on this short sharp ascent.

On finally reaching the broad grassy top, pass to the left of a rocky outcrop ahead; then, continue half-right to a gate in a wire fence. Pass through and on to a broad grass track.

This fine walking path is 'The Street', an old trade and drovers' route across the Border. Used in bygone days, it linked Hownam in Roxburghshire with Alwinton in Upper Coquetdale. It dates from pre-Roman days. On certain old maps it is called Clattering Path. It was used for legal traffic between England and Scotland and no doubt for illegal traffic as well.

(It is at this point that walkers destined for Windy Gyle should turn to the "Greenhill to Windy Gyle" walk – page 101.)

Turn left and follow The Street as it crosses level but rough grass. The Calroust valley lies below to your right. Further on the track crosses small streams which eventually flow into the Calroust Burn. When the track makes a curving descent to the left to a gate in a wire fence, pass through a gate. After a few paces, go through another gate.

The valley to your right leads down to Calroust farm, an escape route should the weather close in. To the right of the valley is Murder Cleugh. How it gained this bloodthirsty name is unknown. Perhaps in the past some traveller met with a gruesome end.

The track then rises and continues parallel to a wire fence on your right. At a fence crossing your path, pass through the gate.

The fence running up to your left leads to a pre-historic hill fort on Blackbrough Hill. To visit the fort, cross over the fence. There is no distinct path so keep parallel with the fence. This will take you to the site of the fort. It is surrounded by an elliptical rampart 100 metres in circumference. To return to the walk, retrace your steps to the track.

Walking past the reservoir in the valley

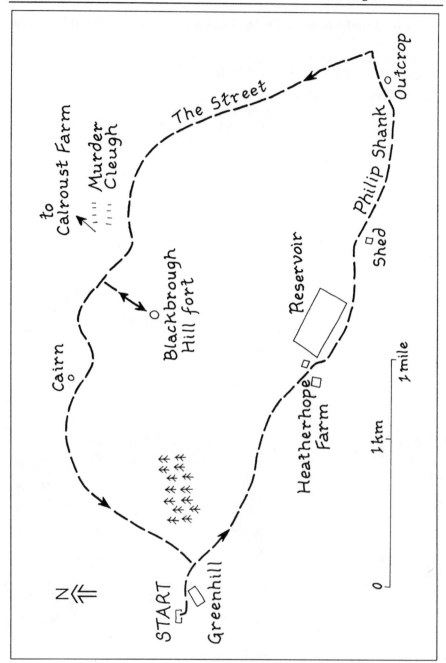

Continue on the track as it begins to descend and, at the lowest point, the wire fence to your right is replaced by a stone wall. A valley can be seen below to your left. Ford a small burn and turn left to descend into this valley. The path is indistinct in places but runs roughly parallel to the burn. Carefully follow it down to a surfaced road and turn right at the road to return to your starting point.

23. Greenhill to Hownam Hill Fort

*A pleasant walk, beginning with a gentle climb soon leading level
ground before descending*

Distance: 6.5km (4 miles)

Grade: Easy

Maps: Ordnance Survey Landranger 80. Ordnance Survey Pathfinder 486
NT61/71. Ordnance Survey Outdoor Leisure 16

Start: At GR788175 on the roadside just before Greenhill Farm

---

Hownam Rings, dating from the sixth century, is the site of a prehistoric
settlement. It contains traces of up to 155 dwellings and provides a
commanding view overlooking the surrounding countryside.

Take the road leading to the left of Greenhill farm to a gate. Pass through
and along a surfaced road until you cross a bridge spanning the Heatherhope
Burn on your left. Approximately a dozen steps on turn left off the road to
follow a narrow grass path which leads up a valley. Ignore the stronger farm
track leading off to the right. The path rises along the side of Headshaw Law
to a stone wall at the head of the valley. Pass through the gate and turn left
on to a broad grassy track which runs parallel to a stone wall. The path gently
rises before levelling out.

> This broad path is an old drovers' road known as The Street. In early
> summer, the grassy slopes crossed by The Street are covered with purple
> and yellow wild pansies, speedwell and tormentil; the songs of the
> skylark and tiny meadow pippet delight the ear.

Continue parallel to the wall on your left until you reach a fork in the path,
before a gate in the wall. Take the right-hand fork directly to the site of
Hownam hill fort, passing The Shearers on the way.

> 'The Shearers' is the name for the line of standing stones stretching
> across the path. Legend has it these are the remains of eleven people
> who worked on a Sunday and were turned into blocks of stone as
> punishment. During excavations of Hownam Rings a flint knife was
> unearthed. This is on display at the Museum of Antiquities at Newcastle
> upon Tyne University. The museum is open to the public and is, at the
> time of writing, free of charge, though welcoming voluntary contribu-

Approaching the hill fort

tions. Many artifacts found on excavation are on display. Some of these were unearthed on or around the Cheviot area.

On leaving the hill fort, retrace your steps. At the gate in the stone wall passed earlier, go through and descend a broad track which eventually passes through a derelict stone wall.

A dozen or so paces past this derelict wall there is an ancient standing stone on a small hillock to the left of the track.

Still descending, pass to the left of an old enclosure planted with coniferous trees. Due to its distinctive shape this is named Horseshoe Plantation on the Ordnance Survey map. Hownam can be seen below and ahead as you go towards the lower edge of the plantation. At a wire fence across the track go through the gate and continue descending to pass to the side of a stone wall. Go through the gate next to a white-painted house and descend on a surfaced road to Hownam.

The village of Hownam is a single row of houses to the side of the road, one of which is the village post office. The village has a church dating back from the twelfth century and it was established by John of Ormiston.

Turn left on reaching the main road to pass the old school and cross the bridge. Soon you reach a fork in the road, take the left fork and follow the road to return to your starting point.

Along this road can be seen metal marker posts bearing the letters 'KWW'. These indicate the route of underground water pipes which ran from Heatherhope reservoir to Kelso, providing a water supply in former years.

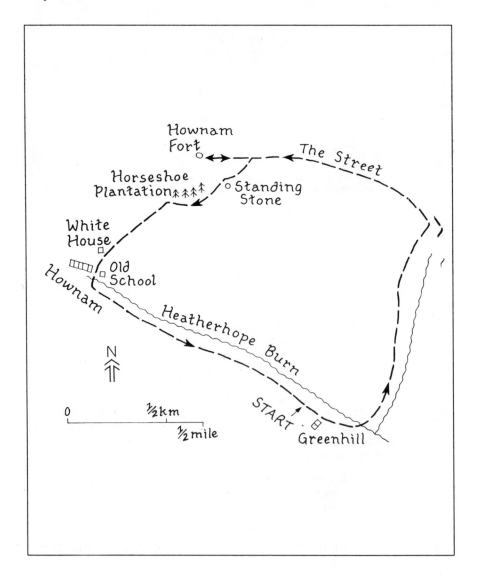

24. Greenhill to Windy Gyle

An alternative Scottish ascent of Windy Gyle, third highest summit in the Cheviots.

Distance: 14.6km (9 miles)

Grade: Strenuous

Maps: Ordnance Survey Landranger 80. Ordnance Survey Pathfinder 487 NT81/91. Ordnance Survey Outdoor Leisure 16

Start: At GR788175 roadside before Greenhill Farm

Proceed as described in the walk 'Heatherhope Valley Circular' — page — 94until you pass through the gate on to The Street from Phillip Shank.

At this point turn right and follow the track known as 'The Street' until it bends sharply right to pass through a gate. Then continue until you encounter a well-trodden path leading off to your left.

This path is the Pennine Way, the brain-child of Tom Stephenson, and was the country's first official long-distance footpath. It was opened on April 24, 1965 and it has proved more popular than Tom Stephenson could ever have envisaged, and is now the M1 of long-distance paths.

Turn left on to the Way and follow it as it leads you into a shallow valley, with a burn at its foot which must be forded.

This area is marked on maps as Foul Step. An aptly-named spot if a crossing is made after a spell of bad weather. The Foul Step Burn is a head-water of the Rowhope Burn which flows into the River Coquet.

The path after Foul Step ascends and contours a slope above a deep valley which drops away to your right. At a wire fence, the Border Fence, turn right and keeping near the fence begin the ascent of Windy Gyle. A stile in the fence marks your crossing point. Cross here and turn right. The path continues to ascend. On reaching a path branching off to the left, continue on this path to the summit.

The view from here is stupendous, a 360 degree panorama with rolling hills in all directions. A worthy culmination to the walk. The summit cairn is surmounted by a stone Ordnance Survey column, one of 20,000 which cover the country. These are now redundant since modern

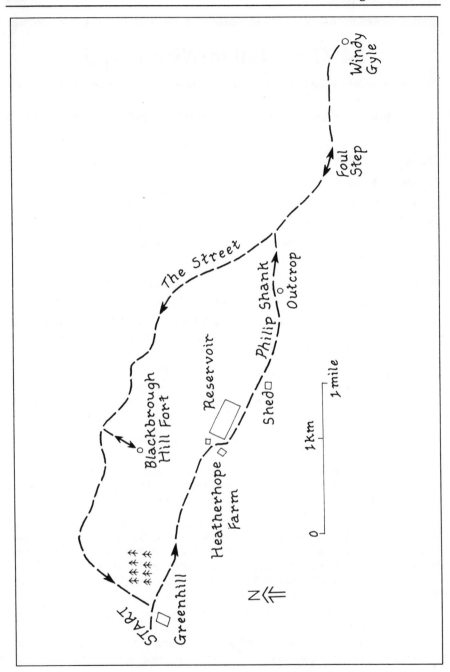

cartography relies upon satellite technology plus observations to compile new maps.

After admiring the view, you have a choice of return routes. You can retrace the route back to the gate leading on to The Street from Phillip Shank, then return to the starting point by passing through the gate and returning the way you came. The second alternative is to turn to the walk named 'Heatherhope Valley Circular' and continue back via The Street. I would advise taking the latter route as this alternative gives even greater variety to this excellent walk.

Miscellaneous Walks in The North Cheviots

This section contains a selection of walks starting from different starting points outside the main valleys. All these walks give you the opportunity to enjoy the lower Cheviot countryside, some with an emphasis on local archeology. Kirk Yetholm has been chosen as a starting point both for its relevance as the end of the Pennine Way and its interesting historic past. It also has a pub, refreshments, and public transport. All important points to consider when out walking.

Walk departure points

High Humbleton: Take the first turning to the left after leaving Wooler on the A697 heading north, signposted Humbleton. A narrow road leads uphill to a T-junction. Turn right and follow the road until you pass the last building on your right. Park on the grass verge next to a gate set in a stone wall to your right. The gate bears a public bridleway sign. GR975284

Kirk Yetholm: There is public transport to the village. Contact Lowland Buses on 01573 24141 for timings. There is ample car parking space within the village. GR827282

Old Yeavering: Leave Wooler heading north on the A697 for 3.3km to Akeld. Turn left here along the B6351 for 3km to a sharp bend to the right. Leave the road here turning left on to a stone track. Please park considerately on the grass verges. GR924303

South Middleton: About 4km south of Wooler on the A697 take a signposted side road for North and South Middleton. A narrow road takes you to a fork. Take the left fork and continue to South Middleton. Pass the farm buildings and houses to a duck pond to the left of the road. There is ample parking space next to it. The ducks and geese here are especially fond of walkers due to their benevolent nature so have some bread ready and donate generously. GR995233

25. Kirk Yetholm and Pennine Way Circular

A gentle valley walk then a return via a ridge walk. An opportunity to walk a small part of the Pennine Way, sampling both the high and low level routes.

Distance: 13.5km (8.5 miles)

Grade: Moderate

Maps: Ordnance Survey Landranger 74. Ordnance Survey Pathfinder 475 NT82/92. Ordnance Survey Outdoor Leisure 16

Start: Bus shelter in Kirk Yetholm. GR827282.

From the bus shelter, take the road signposted for the Halterburn Peniel Revival Centre. This leads up a hill and down the other side to enter the Halterburn Valley.

On the way up the hill, and on the right, you will notice a quaint house painted pink and bearing the name Gypsy Palace. This was once the residence of the royal family of the Faa gypsies and it was here that the last queen, Esther Faa Blythe died in 1883. Yetholm was once the headquarters of the Faa Gypsy and many descendants still live in the village. The last Gypsy king, Charles Faa Blythe, died in 1902. Further on, you will see a wooden seat next to a white cottage. A plaque on the seat reads 'Blessed are those who love the hills'.

Walk along the tarmac road, passing to the left of the Revival centre. The Halter Burn accompanies you as you walk towards Burnhead Farm.

The Peniel Centre was originally a hotel, today it is used as a religious centre for outside activities.

Pass some farm buildings and, just before the farmhouse, turn left as indicated by a Pennine Way signpost leaving the road. Follow a grassy path to cross over a well-made elaborate stile, with steps. Turn right and along a path beside a wire fence, later replaced by a stone wall. The path leads past the farm and to two gates. Pass through and descend to cross a wooden foot bridge spanning the Halter Burn. Turn half-left and up an incline to a tractor track.

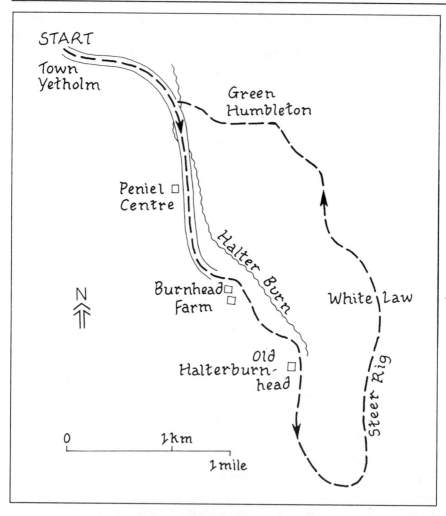

Badgers and foxes have been seen frequently in this area. The above route is new, avoiding close proximity to the farmhouse.

Turn left and along the track. Further on cross a small stream and turn a right-hand corner. Pass to the left of the ruins of Old Halterburnhead set amid trees as derelict as the house.

Old Halterburnhead was once a shepherd's cottage, but was abandoned after a storm blew the top off the building.

Continue past the ruins, keeping close to a stone wall. When the wall ends, go half-right to meet a wire fence. Following beside the fence continue to a Pennine Way marker post. Turn half-left and along the slope of the valley to a stone wall at the head of the valley. Pass through the gate and turn left. The path makes a steep ascent of Steering Knowe. At the top pass through the gate in a wire fence and continue ahead to a Pennine Way signpost.

This signpost bears directions for the high and low level routes of the Pennine Way.

Turn left to follow the high level route as indicated, climbing to a fence junction. Cross the ladder stile and continue along the path which now travels along Steer Rig. After 1.5km the path drops to a saddle.

The wire fence to your right is part of the Border fence, it is your companion along the above stretch.

The path climbs steeply to the top of White Law. From the top, turn left at a fence and follow it across the summit and down the other side. The fence is later replaced by a stone wall. At a ladder stile in the wall, cross over. The path drops steeply before levelling out. Continue to a Pennine Way signpost. Turn half-left here and follow a broad grassy track which descends to the Halter Burn. Ford the burn and turn left to a tarmac road. Turn right and follow the road to return to the start of the walk.

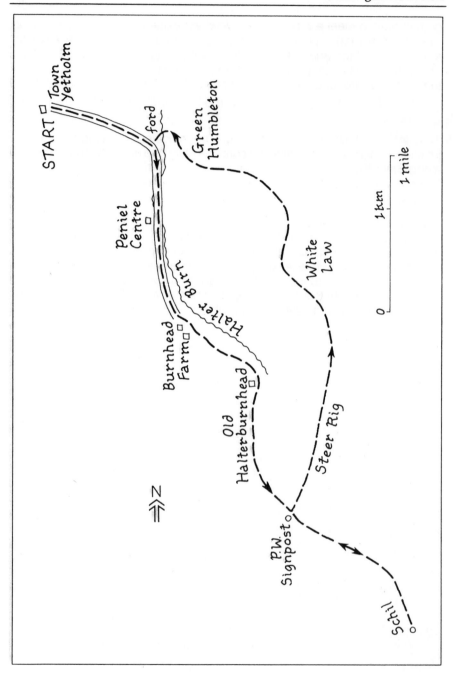

26. Kirk Yetholm to the Schil

Follow the route of the Pennine Way to one of the grandest viewpoints in the Cheviots.

Distance: 16.8km (10.5 miles)

Grade: Moderate

Maps: Ordnance Survey Landranger 74. Ordnance Survey Pathfinder 475 NT82/92. Ordnance Survey Outdoor Leisure 16

Start: At the bus shelter in Kirk Yetholm. GR827282.

Proceed as for the previous 'Kirk Yetholm and Pennine Way Circular' until you reach the Pennine Way signpost at the top of Steering Knowe.

This signpost bears directions for the Pennine Way high level and low level routes.

The Border Fence on the approach to the Schil

From here, turn right, away from the signpost, and follow a grass path as indicated by the Pennine Way arm of the signpost. At a fork in the path, continue on a broad track branching off to your right. Walk on to a dry stone wall and cross over using the ladder stile.

The wall is part of the Border fence. A signpost beside the stile bears directions for the Pennine Way, Kirk Yetholm, Mounthooly and the Schil.

Once across the wall turn right and proceed to a wire fence across the path. Cross via the stile and continue as the path begins to ascend the Schil. The wall has been replaced by a wire fence. Follow alongside this fence to the summit of the Schil.

The actual summit pinnacle is on the other side of the fence. This is best crossed at the point where it bends sharp right. The pinnacle and summit cairn are a short distance ahead.

To return, retrace your steps to the Pennine Way signpost at the top of Steering Knowe. Here there is a choice of return routes. Either return the way you came or use the Pennine Way high-level route. Details of which can be found in the 'Kirk Yetholm and Pennine Way Circular' walk.

27. High Humbleton to Gleadscleugh and Gains Law

A walk into Cheviot country, level most of the way with only one climb. Excellent views.

Distance: 10km (6 miles)

Grade: Easy

Maps: Ordnance Survey Landranger 75. Ordnance Survey 475 NT82/92. Ordnance Survey Outdoor Leisure 16

Start: Gate set in wall after the last building in Humbleton. GR975284.

Pass through the gate bearing a public footpath sign in the stone wall to the right of the road. After 75 metres, pass through another gate. Continue, ignore a track leading off right, until you reach a wooden marker post. Turn right here taking the lesser path indicated by a blue arrow. At the next marker post turn half-right to descend a slight slope and reach the next post just before a stone wall. Turn left and continue along with the wall on your right. At the end of the wall, pass through the gate to your right and turn left. The path runs parallel to a stone wall.

On September 13, 1402, this area was the site of a battle between the Scottish and English forces. Scottish troops, under the command of Archibald, Earl of Douglas, were returning from a raiding party into Northumberland when they discovered a large English force, under the command of Henry Percy, were lying in wait for them at Milfield. The Scots took up defensive positions on the slopes of Humbleton Hill and awaited the English attack.

When the English arrived, instead of mounting a frontal attack, Henry Percy, under the advice of the Earl of March, ordered his archers to fire upon the hill. Volley after volley of arrows rose into the air and descended on the Scots with devastating effect. Hundreds died under this relentless downpour and it was said that many of the dead bristled like hedgehogs.

The Scots fled, utterly routed, and fought their way past Akeld and on to the safety of the Scottish border. Out of 10,000 Scots, some 800 were killed and another 500 perished while crossing the Tweed.

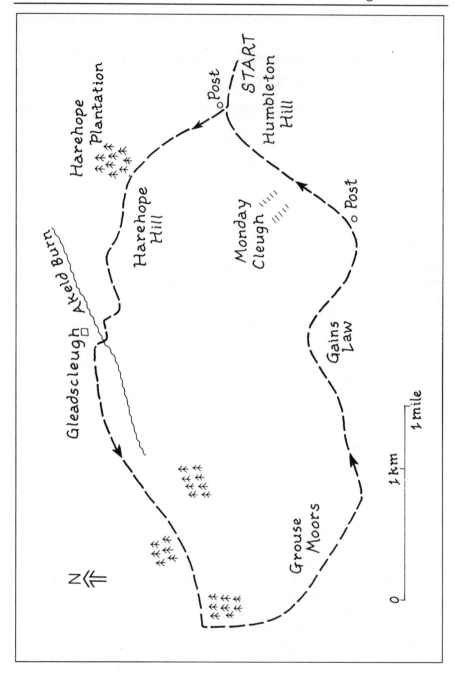

Archibald lost an eye in the battle and was captured. This battle later formed part of the opening scenes from Shakespeare's 'Henry V'.

The path reaches another marker post bearing a blue arrow. Ascend slightly to a gate set in a stone wall. Cross using the stile. The path ascends Harehope Hill to a gate in a stone wall. Pass through, and continue contouring around the hill. Soon you can see the hamlet of Akeld below.

The view across the Milfield Plain is stupendous, stretching to the distant hills in Scotland. Akeld was once a much larger village in medieval times. Today only the farmhouse and cottages remain. Part of the hamlet has been modified to contain a holiday complex.

The path now begins to descend the hillside towards a stone wall. At this wall, turn left and walk parallel to it over level ground. Soon the buildings of Gleadscleugh appear. At the end of the wall pass through a gate and turn right.

Gleadscleugh was an old shepherd's house but is now used as a holiday retreat.

On meeting a fence across the path use the stile to cross and turn half-left to walk over rough ground and reach a farm track. Turn left on to the track and follow it as it descends to cross Akeld Burn and climb up the other side to a gate in a wire fence. Go through the gate.

At the gate is a sign stating 'Please take care. Some of the ground nesting birds that breed here during the spring are easily disturbed by people and more so by dogs. During April, May, June you can help minimise such disturbance by keeping dogs on a lead and keeping to the paths. Your cooperation is much appreciated. Enjoy your visit'. This is good advice!

The track climbs steeply before levelling out. It then travels along the upper side of Akeld Valley to a fence across the path. Go through the gate and then along the side of a plantation.

Looking across the valley to your left, there is a square-shaped plantation enclosed by a stone wall. Looking ahead, Cheviot is never long out of sight.

Continue along the stone track to pass another plantation and then through a gate. Once through the gate turn left and continue on a stone track taking you parallel to a plantation. At a gate pass through and a dozen paces on you will reach a marker post. Turn left as indicated, leaving the track and crossing heather moor. Pass to the right of a large stone cairn.

These are grouse shooting moors, common sense and sensitivity should be used during the shooting season. The heather, which the grouse feed on, is carefully managed for the birds' benefit. At regular intervals large sections of the heather are burnt off to produce juicy new shoots which the grouse prefer. The unburnt sections are ideal for nesting among the taller plants.

At a marker post just before a stone wall turn left and continue along with the wall to your right. Go through the gate in a fence.

Looking to the left, the view of the Milfield Plain has opened up again.

Continue over heather moor to a gate in the stone wall, pass through it. Walk on with the wall on your left. At the end of the wall there is a marker post. Continue ahead until you reach a wire fence. The path turns left to run alongside it for a few paces before reaching a stile. Cross over and follow a path which leads to a stone wall and then runs parallel to it. Pass by a marker post and continue to contour Gains Law. Later the path descends to a marker post. Turn left here and descend to a gate. Go through and continue descending to a further marker post.

To the right of this post there are several paths which lead to the summit of Humbleton Hill. This allows closer inspection of the extensive hill fort. None of these paths are public footpaths or rights of way. So, if access is desired, it would be courteous to seek permission first from the local farmer before using them.

Go to the left of the marker post and gently descend around the lower slopes of Humbleton Hill. Pass through a gate and, at the next marker post, turn right as indicated by a blue arrow and follow the track to return to your starting point.

28. South Middleton to Threestoneburn Woods

A pleasant walk over level ground

Distance: 11km (7 miles)

Grade: Easy

Maps: Ordnance Survey Landrangers 75 and 81. Ordnance Survey Pathfinders 475 NT82/92 and 487 NT81/91. Ordnance Survey Outdoor Leisure 16

Start: At the duck pond in South Middleton. GR995233.

The stone circle at Threestoneburn Wood is believed to be of ceremonial significance. It dates back from 1600-1500 BC.

From the duck pond, take the stone track signposted for S. Middleton, Dodd and Threestoneburn. The track rises gently to cross a cattle grid and continues to where the fence on your right ends. At this point there is a fork in the track, take the right fork and continue to a stone wall across the track. Pass through the gate and ascend slightly to pass to the left of a plantation. Just before another stone wall the track again forks. Take the lesser grass path to the right and after a few paces cross a ladder stile over a stone wall.

The stile has two marker arrows. The one bearing left leads to the cottage of South Middleton moor.

After crossing the stile turn half-left on a grassy path to pass to the left of a sheep fold and through a gate in a wire fence. After passing through the gate turn half-left towards the plantation ahead.

Looking to your left and slightly ahead, you can see the distinctive outline of Middleton Crags against the skyline.

At the plantation a stile leads into the trees, a yellow arrow indicating the way. Continue to descend into a hollow, where another stile in the fence allows exit from the trees. Climb out of the hollow up to a stile in a wire fence above. Cross over and turn half-right to a marker post next to a good farm track. Turn left and follow the track to a gate. Pass through this and continue on the track; this rises gently to the lower slopes of Middleton Crags and then curves left around the base.

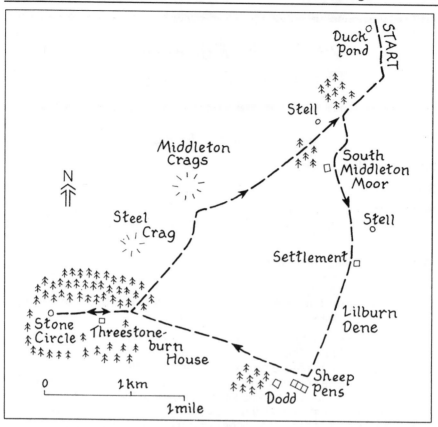

The wheatear can be found on moors and heaths. It is one of our earliest visitors, arriving towards the end of March after over-wintering in Africa.

You reach a point where the track turns right and climbs towards the top of the crags. Leave the track and continue straight ahead over a less distinct grassy path. Pass through a gate in a fence and walk on to a large plantation. A gate allows you to enter.

This is Threestoneburn Wood, a coniferous plantation covering many acres. Today, there is now more forestry in this country than at any other time in the last thousand years. However oak and hazel are dying off quicker than they are being reproduced and without the assistance of man they could become extinct.

A broad heather-lined track passes between the trees to exit by a stile in a fence ahead and below. After the stile walk on a few paces to a good farm track and a wooden marker post. Turn right and on to pass through a gate and down a track edged with various species of trees to your left to Threestoneburn House.

The house is used as a holiday retreat. Before this it was a shooting lodge.

The track leads right of the house towards a wooden foot bridge spanning the Threestone Burn. Cross over and bear half-right. Walk along a grassy path to pass through a gate in a wire fence. Cross over another foot bridge and walk on to a stone wall.

These foot bridges were built by National Park Voluntary Wardens.

Pass through a gate in the wall and turn left. Ford a small burn and continue to the site of the Threestonburn stone circle.

The circle is thought to have been of ceremonial use. Only three of the original stones are still standing. The rest lie scattered around.

Retrace your steps back to Threestoneburn House and back along the tree-lined path to the marker post passed earlier. Continue straight on ahead to pass through a gate and along a forest track between the trees. At a fence across the track pass through the gate and exit from the plantation. Continue along the track to a foot bridge spanning the Threestone Burn which has accompanied you on your right.

This foot bridge was built in 1981 by the National Parks Voluntary Warden Service.

Cross the bridge and turn left along a broad track which is soon joined by a forestry road coming in from the right. Continue to pass to the left of a small plantation. Just after this, the Dodd farmstead is seen to your right. A dozen paces on, next to sheep pens, is a signpost.

This post bears directions for Threestoneburn House and Langlee in one direction, S. Middleton moor and S. Middleton in the other.

Turn left at the signpost and head across rough moor, as indicated by the direction arm for South Middleton. Aim towards a rock outcrop with a marker post to the right of it. From this post, continue past to another marker post, The path then descends a slope to a wire fence, which you cross via the stile provided. Turn left, as indicated by a yellow marker arrow, and descend into the beautiful Lilburn Dene.

This dene is really pleasant. It has the Lilburn Burn gargling over stones down the middle lined with alder trees. It eventually flows into the River Till.

Cross the bridge then, ascending a grassy path, climb out of the dene. At the top, the path passes to the left of a stone enclosure. The path then dips into a small hollow with a burn at the bottom. A plank bridge enables you to cross. The path rises to a marker post. Continue along the path aided by further marker posts.

The track passes to the left of a prehistoric settlement. Earth ridges and hollows can be seen quite clearly.

Continue to the next marker post, the path gradually deteriorating. Keep straight on and, using the marker posts, cross a rough stretch to the final post.

Head in the direction of the right side of a plantation ahead. To the right of this plantation the brilliant yellow of gorse bushes form a reliable beacon, when in bloom.

After the final post, the path dips into Middleton Dene. Across the dene is the cottage of South Middleton moor. Follow the path into the dene and cross the burn via the wooden foot bridge. Ascend to pass to the right of the cottage. Just after the cottage is a marker post. Take the right-hand path which leads up to a gate in a stone wall. Do not go through, turn left and keeping parallel to the wall reach a fence across the path. Go through the gate and continue alongside the wall until you reach a gate in the wall. Pass through on to a farm track. Follow the track to return to your starting point.

The bridge at Lilburn Dene

29. Old Yeavering to the College Burn

A gentle walk suitable for families and those just wishing to amble along.

Distance: 9km (5.5 miles)

Grade: Easy

Maps: Ordnance Survey Landranger 74. Ordnance Survey Pathfinders NT83/93 and 475 NT82/92. Ordnance Survey Outdoor Leisure 16

Start: Grass verge of track leading to Old Yeavering. GR924303.

From your parking spot, walk up the stone track to pass to the left of the cottages of Old Yeavering. Pass through the metal gate, to the right of which is a signpost bearing directions for Commonburn House and Hethpool. Keep to the track as it bends right and crosses a small burn. The track then bends to the left and goes through a gate before contouring along the side of a valley to a stone wall across the track.

To your left stands Yeavering Bell. Its lower slopes are dotted with gorse bushes, resplendent in summer with their small yellow flowers.

Pass through a gap in the wall and over an old cattle grid. Then, keeping on the track, reach another wall across the track. Cross another cattle grid and on a few steps to a wooden marker post. Continue past the post along the stone track to pass through a gate. Walk quietly past the steading at Torleehouse. Here the track swings to the right and behind the house. At this point leave the track where it bends and climb a small slope to a gate in a wire fence.

Torleehouse was originally known as 'Tarleazes' meaning a clearing on a hill.

Pass through the gate and continue to another gate leading into a plantation. Cross the stile to the right of the gate and down a broad avenue between the trees. Leave the plantation through another gate and then descend on a track leading towards the College Valley.

Looking to your right, the tree-lined route of the College Burn can be

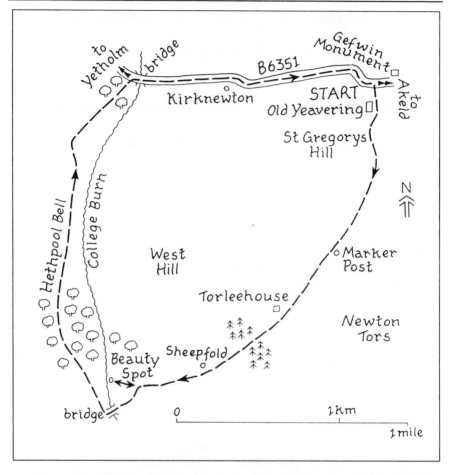

discerned. Ahead, amid some trees, is the small hamlet of Hethpool. To your left rises the flank of Newton Tors.

At a stone sheep fold you will see a wooden marker post. Turn half-right here and cross rough ground to a stile in a wire fence. Cross over the fence and turn left to descend into a small valley with a burn at the bottom. Ford the burn and turn right to ascend back out of the valley.

Beware the gorse bushes on the descent and ascent of this valley. They hang dangerously close to the path and their thorns are lethal. The burn is a small tributary feeding into the College Burn.

Continue past a marker post, keeping a wire fence to your left and the valley to your right.

Feral Cheviot goats can sometimes be seen feeding on the rough land to your left. Here, I once saw two goats feeding in the grass before going off to some trees where they began to strip the bark for a tasty ending to their meal.

The path soon makes a steep descent into the College Valley where on reaching the bottom cross the stile in the wire fence to your left.

Incidentally, a slight detour to the right instead of crossing the stile leads down to a beauty spot beside the College Burn. This is an ideal spot to have a soothing rest or a picnic.

The lower reaches of the College Burn

After crossing the stile the path winds through ferns and trees to a wooden foot bridge spanning the College Burn. Cross the bridge and at the end pass through the gate and turn left to follow the path up a gentle slope. Join a path coming in from the right, which climbs and then contours around Hethpool Bell, passing over stiles as you go.

The sides of the Bell are covered by bracken. The National Park is planting new oak trees to replace some older oaks planted by Lord Collingwood. Sheep have been excluded from this area to allow the regeneration of the oaks. The management plan should show a great improvement for the next generations to appreciate.

The path curves around the hill and then rises to a wire fence and runs parallel to it. At a stile cross over and turn right to continue along a grass path over open ground. When you reach the end of the fence, the path drops quite steeply to the floor of the valley. Descend with care, especially after wet weather.

The College Burn owes its name to the two Saxon words, *col* and *leche*, meaning a stream running through boggy land.

At the bottom of the incline, take the path leading off left. This takes you along the valley floor through gorse bushes and over rock strewn ground with the burn to your right. The area is alive with rabbits. Where the path forks, take the right fork to a wire fence. Go through the gate and continue with the burn still on your right. Pass a marker post and continue to the next one. Turn left here and up a small slope. Just before a gate in a stone wall turn right and walk along beside the wall to a ladder stile. Cross over and turn right. Keep beside the wire fence till you reach a stile, cross over. A path takes you through trees to emerge on a surfaced road. Turn right and on to Kirknewton.

Kirknewton is a quiet village first mentioned in 1336 when it was known as New Town. It suffered badly during the 16th century from Border warfare. The village church, St Gregory's, dates from the 13th century. Inside the church is a carving of the Virgin and Magi. This is curious, in that the Magi are depicted as wearing kilts. The churchyard holds the grave of Josephine Butler, a famous Victorian social reformer who died in 1906.

Once past the village, remain on the surfaced road as it takes you back to your starting point.

Section 2:
The Southern Cheviots

This section describes walks in the southern hills and the Coquet Valley. There are several possible access points, and some of these are listed below. Firstly, however, a few words of warning are in order.

MOD land – a warning!

The land to the south of the River Coquet in Upper Coquetdale is owned by the Ministry of defence and forms part of the Otterburn Training Ranges. Due to some parts of the area being used for the firing of live ammunition, it is off limits to the public for most of the year. When red flags are displayed the range is in use and entry is forbidden. However, when the flags are not flying, additional access land and military roads are open to the public and a much better view of this unique area is

A timely reminder!

possible. Leaflets are available from National Park Information Offices. Further details can be obtained by contacting the Range Officer on 01830-520569.

It must be stressed how dangerous it is to wander from recognised routes as live ammunition or unexploded shells could be fatal if wrongly handled. Never touch any suspicious object.

Troops from Britain and NATO undergo training in combat conditions on these ranges. NATO and UK air forces also use the ranges to practice air-to-ground missile attacks and war games.

The land to the north of the River Coquet as far as the Border fence is also used by the military but this is a 'dry' training area, in that no live ammunition is used. There are many public rights of way distributed across this area and walkers may use them at any time of the year with no restrictions on access. However, you should be aware of the likelihood of meeting soldiers and military vehicles.

The Otterburn Training Ranges were initiated in 1911 as an artillery range for the Territorial Arms. During World War Two the ranges were extended and today it is the largest live firing range in the country. The present range covers an area of 58,000 acres and lies within the Northumberland National Park.

Walk departure points

Prendwick: Parking on the grass verge to the side of the road south of Prendwick Farm. GR003122. Please park considerately.

Alnham: Parking on the grass verge of the road outside Alnham Church. Post Bus from Alnwick. Contact Alnwick Post Office for times.

Biddlestone: Parking on grass verge of road next to the telephone box. GR961083. Post Bus from Rothbury. Contact Rothbury Post Office for times.

Alwinton: Public car park in village with toilet facilities and information board. Post Bus service from Rothbury and Alnwick. Contact respective post office.

Barrowburn: Public car park at Wedder Loup just south of Barrowburn farm. GR866103. No public transport.

Blindburn: Car park at Buckhams Walls Bridge to west of Blindburn farm. GR830109. No public transport available. Information board.

Shilmoor: On grass verge to right of road before metal bridge spanning the River Coquet. No public transport available. Please park well off the road. GR886075.

Tow Ford: On grass verge to side of road east of the Tow ford. GR762134. No public transport available.

30. Alnham to Pigdon's Leap

A delightful walk following part of an old smuggling route and visiting a pretty waterfall.

Distance: 11km (7 miles)

Grade: Moderate

Maps: Ordnance Survey Landranger 81. Ordnance Survey Pathfinder 487 NT81/91. Ordnance Survey Outdoor Leisure 16.

Start: On the grass verges of the road next to Alnham Church. GR993109.

Proceed up the road with Alnham Church on your right until you reach a signpost to the right of the road. This bears directions for Bleakhope and Shank House. Leave the road, turning right, follow a grassy track between a stone wall on your right and trees on your left. At a gate across the track pass through and walk on as the track climbs a short steep rise. Pass through another gate and remain on the track with a stone wall on your left and a plantation on your right.

> The buildings of Castlehill Farm are to your right. Most dry stone walls were built in the 18th and 19th centuries. They have a life expectancy of around 200 years.

At the end of the plantation pass through a gate in a wooden fence running across the track. Continue with another plantation to your left.

> This plantation comprises a mixture of deciduous trees interspersed with occasional Scots Pine and underplanted with rhododendron bushes. A plaque in the wire fence surrounding the plantation bears the date 1905, this presumably being the year when the forest was planted.

When the plantation ends, continue, keeping the stone wall to your left and climbing onwards to reach a gate. Go through the gate and bear half-right towards a red stone track which is visible ahead close to the top of the rise. At the track turn left and follow it as it climbs.

> The view is spectacular on a clear day with the Vale of Whittingham plainly visible and the distant Simonside Hills above Rothbury etched on the horizon.

At the top, look for a wooden marker post. Here, leave the track, which now

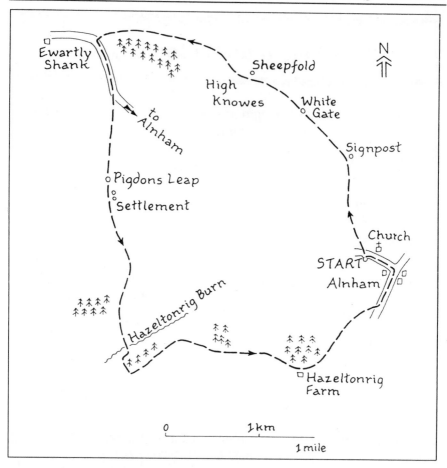

bends to the right, and keeping straight ahead on a broad grassy path, pass to the left of the marker post.

This is Salters Road. In olden times when meat could only be preserved by salting or smoking, salt was a valuable item. This route was used by traders carrying salt from the coastal salt pans to Scotland. Before this, the route was known as Theeves Rode and was used by smugglers transporting illicit whisky across the border.

Remain on the path until you meet a dry stone wall which you will cross via the stile next to the gate. On maps this is marked as White Gate. The stile bears two marker arrows; one points left to Alnham, but you take the other direction. Once over the stile bear half-right and continue along the path to pass to the left of a stone sheep fold. The path now begins its ascent of the lower slope of High Knowes. At a fork, take the right-hand path to a gate in a wire fence.

On the summit of High Knowes the remains of ancient settlements have been found dating back from 1800 BC. Excavations revealed the site of a homestead with two large and two small houses within an enclosure. Further excavations 90 metres away from this site located a further homestead dating from the early Iron Age.

Pass through the gate and continue along the path to reach the corner of a plantation. The path runs parallel and to the right of the trees, composed mainly of Scots Pine, to reach a gate. Pass through the gate and descend a short slope to reach a surfaced road.

Looking right, the farm buildings of Ewartly Shank are visible. This is a sheep stock farm. On early maps it is marked as Elsdon Shank.

Turn left and walk along the road until you reach a gate and cattle grid. Cross the grid and immediately turn right to drop into a small dip before rising to follow a broad grassy path. Continue on the path, keeping a wire fence visible off to your right. When you reach a fork in the path, take the right-hand one. The path soon begins to bend left and pass through bracken. It then curves right to reach a gate in a wire fence. Pass through the gate and descend into a gorge created by the Spartly Burn below. Descend to the burn.

This is Pigdon's Leap, it is totally unexpected with its waterfalls, ferns and green covered boulders. Pause here a while to appreciate its simple beauty. Pigdon's Leap earned its name to a border cattle lifter named Pigdon. Hotly pursued by his enemies and cornered he leapt across the gorge and thus escaped meeting his threatened end.

Ford the burn and follow a path rising out of the gorge. The stones and earthworks above are the remains of an ancient settlement. Pass through the scattered stones and over rough grass on an indistinct path aiming towards the lower left slope of the hill ahead. When a wire fence becomes visible off to your left angle towards it and continue to reach a gate in this fence. Go through the gate and follow a distinct broad grassy path which takes you around the lower slope of Hazeltonrig Hill. The path curves to pass to the left of a plantation before descending to the Hazeltonrig Burn. Ford the burn then up the slope to reach a plantation.

According to the Ordnance Survey maps there should be a public footpath through this plantation. The plantation is surrounded by a wire fence with the trees so densely packed that you would need the cunning of a fox, the agility of a weasel and the height of a rabbit to get through. As most of us do not have these attributes I suggest, you turn right and along the side of the plantation to reach a gate. Pass through this gate and turn sharp left parallel to the plantation to reach a yellow arrowed marker post, you are then back on the public right of way. This diversion is not a public right of way but, according to advice on rights of way issued by the Ramblers Association, if the way is blocked you are advised to seek the nearest possible route around the obstacle returning to the legal right of way as soon as possible.

Turn left at the marker post and immediately through a gate. Follow the path across good pasture walking slightly to the left to reach a gate in the wire fence ahead. The plantation is on your left. Pass through the gate and on to reach the next gate. Pass through this gate and turn half-right to cross pasture land towards the right-hand corner of another plantation ahead. Pass by the corner and turn left along the side of the trees to reach a gate in a wire fence. Pass through and bear half-right to descend a slope. As you descend the buildings of Hazeltonrig Farm become visible ahead. Continue to descend, making your way towards the trees to the left of the farm. Cross over a farm road and through a gate leading into the trees. Once through a path takes you to Hazeltonrig Burn.

This is a wide burn so it's fortunate that a wooden foot bridge has been built to allow you across without getting your feet wet.

Cross the bridge and on to a stone track. Soon a grassy path leads off left. Leave the track here and follow the path as it takes you behind the buildings and then up a steep incline to reach a gate. Pass through the gate and turn half-left across pasture to reach another gate. Go through and walk on to reach the next gate. Pass through and walk on with a wire fence to your left until another gate takes you into another field with a stone wall to your left. Keep parallel to the wall as the path leads you to a surfaced road. Turn left and follow the road to return to Biddlestone and the start of your walk.

31. Alnham to Alnhammoor via Salters Road

A walk along part of a historic trading and smuggling route.

Distance: 11.5km (7 miles)

Grade: Moderate

Maps: Ordnance Survey Landranger 81. Ordnance Survey Pathfinder 487 NT81/91. Ordnance Survey Outdoor Leisure 16.

Start: Grass verges of road beside Alnham Church. GR993109.

Walk up the road with the church to your right until you reach a signpost to the right of the road. Leave the road here and turn right to follow a grassy path through trees to reach a gate. Pass through the gate and walk on as the path climbs a short steep rise. Pass through the next gate and keep on the path with a stone wall to your left and a plantation to your right. Remain on the path to reach a gate which you pass through. Turn half-right and head towards a red stone track which is visible ahead close to the top of the rise. At the track turn left and follow as it climbs to reach a wooden marker post. Turn left, leaving the track and follow a broad grassy path, this is Salters Road. Follow the track to ford a small burn and then reach a stone wall with a gate. Cross via the stile to the side of the gate.

On maps this point is marked as 'White gate', but is in fact a metal gate which is painted blue. A point of interest regarding stone walls. If you choose to rest by a stone wall take note of any small burrows or entrances in the wall face as they could conceal an adder or a weasel, both of which may inflict a nasty bite if disturbed or frightened. Though adders are venomous their bite is generally non-fatal. However, if bitten, keep calm and seek medical help quickly. An anti-histamine will normally be prescribed. Dogs however are more susceptible, a bite in this case may often prove fatal. Another reason for keeping your dog on a lead whilst walking.

There are marker arrows on the gate, our route takes us to the right. After about half a kilometre, the path passes to the left of a stone sheep fold. It then contours around the side of High Knowes. At a fork in the track take the right-hand turning which will take you to a wire fence. Pass through the gate

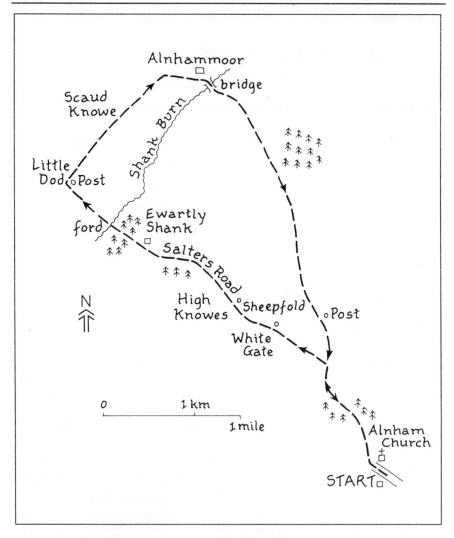

and follow the path as it leads you to a plantation and along the side of it. Pass through the gate and make the slight descent to the farm road. Turn right and follow the road to reach Ewartly Shank.

On 19th century and earlier maps the farm is marked as Elsdon Shank. On the summit of High Knowes are the remains of a palisaded settlement dating from about 1800 BC, but it is not easily discernible. A palisaded settlement comprised of a cluster of circular wooden huts surrounded by a wooden stockade.

Pass in front of the bungalow then left to reach a wooden gate. Pass through the gate and left again to reach a stile crossing the fence to your right. Cross the stile and then turn left to reach a gate leading into a plantation. Pass through the trees to reach another gate which allows you to exit from the trees. Descend into a valley via a path leading to a ford across the burn. Head towards a gate in the fence above climbing out of the valley and climb towards the top of Little Dod.

Some way up there is a cairn to the left of the path which should not be mistaken for the summit as there is still a little way to go yet. The summit itself is quite flat and has no cairn (as yet).

Cross the summit and descend to reach a small cairn of stones around a marker post. Turn right here, as indicated by a yellow arrow. The path contours around the slope of Scaud Knowe and is clearly marked by wooden marker posts with yellow arrows.

There are some fine views from this path including that of Cheviot, the Northumbrian coastal plain and to the right the Simonside Hills etched against the skyline. Behind Little Dod rises Hogden Law with its distinctive summit cairn.

Soon the farm of Alnhammoor appears ahead, the path descending to a wire fence. Go through the gate and along a path which gradually veers right and down into a shallow valley. Continue to reach a plank bridge spanning a narrow burn. Cross and climb the path ahead, ignoring a tractor track leading off to the left. The path rises to a wire fence crossed via a ladder stile. A grass path leads behind the farm buildings to a stone wall. Continue along beside the wall and descend to reach a metal gate. Pass through and cross the burn via a wooden foot bridge.

The Shank Burn flows into the River Breamish a little to the southeast of Alnhammoor.

Follow the track to a gate and use the stile to cross over. Walk half-right over a grassy path towards a gate in the top right-hand corner of the field. Pass through the gate and follow a broad track which rises gently. There is a wire fence to your left.

This track can be very muddy after a spell of wet weather.

Later the fence turns away left from the track but you continue rising to reach the top corner of a plantation. Here the path dips sharply to ford a small burn before rising to a gate.

On the ascent, you see the farm at Alnhammoor below. On the horizon, Great Staindrop is to the right and to the left the dome of Hedgehope Hill. Behind and to the left of it rises Cheviot.

Cross the stile and keeping a wire fence to your right walk uphill for about

300m before veering half-left to contour around the lower slopes of the hill. After rounding the hill the path travels over rough ground for about one kilometre to reach a wire fence.

The above can be a difficult stretch as the path is not clear due to the rough nature of the land. As a rough guide I would advise keeping the wire fence to your right at about a distance of 300m and walking parallel to it. Eventually you will reach the wire fence described above.

At the fence turn left and continue along beside it until you reach a gate set in the fence. Pass through the gate and follow a broad farm track which curves left and then right as it contours around Hart Law.

Below can be seen the spread of the Vale of Whittingham and the Simonside Hills on the horizon.

At a wooden marker post to the right of the track turn left and descend, retracing your steps as at the beginning of the walk, to return to Alnham and the start of the walk.

The church at Alnham is dedicated to St Michael. It was renovated in 1870 and the font is dated 1664. In the 12th century it belonged to the monks of Alnwick Abbey. The Vicar's Pele next to the church is mentioned in the Border Survey of 1415. In the late 1650s it was left to decay but was restored in the early 1800s. From the 1950s to 1960s it was used as a youth hostel. Today it is in private ownership.

32. Alwinton to Kidlandlee

Part country, part forest, combining the best of Cheviot countryside.

Distance: 9.6km (6 miles)

Grade: Moderate

Maps: Ordnance Survey Landranger 80. Ordnance Survey Pathfinder 499 80/90. Ordnance Survey Outdoor Leisure 16.

Start: Alwinton car park GR919063.

Leave the car park turning left to pass the houses on the village street. Where the road bends to the right walk straight ahead towards a wooden foot bridge spanning a burn. Cross the bridge before turning left along a surfaced road ignoring a turning left leading to some farm buildings. The road soon peters out to become a stony track which climbs towards a gate in a stone wall

Alwinton village

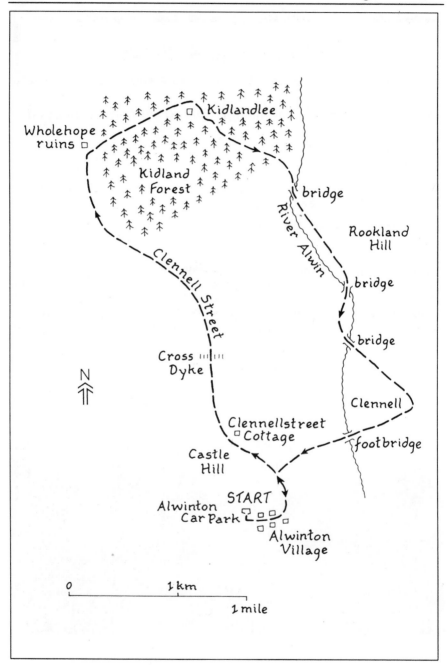

Wholehope ruins

Kidlandlee

Kidland Forest

River Alwin

bridge

Rookland Hill

Clennell Street

bridge

bridge

Cross Dyke

Clennell

Clennellstreet Cottage

footbridge

Castle Hill

START

Alwinton Car Park

Alwinton Village

N

0   1 km

1 mile

crossing the track. Pass through the gate and continue upwards passing to the left of the cottage of Clennellstreet.

The track you are on is an ancient drove road known as Clennell Street. It runs from Alwinton to Hownam in Scotland, a distance of 19km. In medieval times it was a popular route for smugglers of illicit whisky and the movement of livestock, both legal and illegal, across the border. Today it forms an ideal route for walkers.

After passing the cottage the track splits but a wooden marker post bearing directions arrows aids navigation. Take the left path indicated by a blue arrow which gradually rises towards a wire fence and then runs parallel to it. After about half a kilometre the path dips at a point known as Cross Dyke.

The purpose of the cross dyke was to block or delay passage along this ancient drove road. The dyke would slow down raiding parties fleeing with stolen cattle or sheep and allow their pursuers to catch them and deal out suitable punishment.

The path again begins to climb and crosses over the summit of the hill. Ahead can be seen the extensive plantations of Kidland Forest. The path, now descending, soon reaches a wire fence. Pass through the gate and cross a wet patch before bending to the right and climbing a small rise. The path contours the side of Uplaw Knowe before running parallel to the fence bordering Kidland Forest on your right.

Kidland Forest is one of the larger plantations within the Cheviots. Most of the trees within Kidland were planted between 1950 and 1970. Looking at it is not surprising that today there is more land covered by trees in this country then at any other time in the past 1000 years. Sadly however, oak and hazel are dying off quicker than they are being reproduced and without mans help could soon become extinct.

Pass to the right of some sheep pens and then parallel to a fence on your left to reach a gate across the path. Go through the gate and continue along the path until you reach a fork in the path. Take the right-hand fork and continue with the forest on your right. At a gate across the path go through and up the slope ahead to reach the ruins of Wholehope.

Wholehope is today a pile of ruins. Originally used as a shepherd's house it was later modified to become a youth hostel. This later closed down in the 1960s and the place was abandoned and just left to decay.

Turn right just before the ruins and pass through a gate in the wire fence to your left just past the remains of the cottage. Once through the gate the path drops steeply into a gully to cross a burn before climbing out again. Your route is then across rough moorland to a stone wall to the left of the moor allowing you access into Kidland Forest.

Any difficulties in fording the above burn can be removed by travelling a short distance downstream where the crossing is easier then walking back up to regain the path.

Pass through the gate into the forest turning right as indicated by a yellow arrow and a dozen paces on reach a forest road. Turn right along the road and follow it for 100m at which point it bends right. At this juncture leave the path continuing straight ahead up a grassy break between the trees. At the top of the rise continue, keeping a wire fence to your right. When the fence ends a yellow arrow on the last post alerts you to turn right. Walk on between the trees as the path bends left and on to reach a stone cairn topped by a marker post. Walk straight ahead through the trees on a narrow path as indicated at the marker post, ignore the lesser path leading off half-left. Continue through the trees to reach a wire fence. Cross via the stile provided on to grass pasture and Kidlandlee Farm.

> Kidlandlee House was built at the turn of the last century as a summer residence and shooting lodge for Captain Leyland of Haggerston Castle, near Berwick.

After crossing the stile turn left and continue between two stone walls until you reach a gate in the stone wall to your right. Pass through this gate turning half-left to pass through the farm buildings and reach another gate.

> Please walk quietly through the farm keeping any dogs firmly under control.

Pass through the gate thus exiting from the farm enclosure and follow a stone track which curves right to take you to a gate set in a stone wall. Pass through the gate and descend a stone track with a wire fence to your right and trees to your left. At a point where the track bends right leave the track and turn left towards a stile in a wire fence. Cross the stile and walk down the side of a grass field parallel to trees on your left.

> Notice the raised grass square to your right.

At a fence across your path use the stile to cross over. A narrow path leads you between trees to descend gently to a fork in the path. Take the right fork and follow the path as it continues through trees, now descending more steeply. At a red stoned forestry road cross over and remain on the path as it descends quite steeply to reach another forestry road at the bottom of the descent. Turn right and after a few paces cross over a cattle grid. Continue on the surfaced road as it takes you down the Alwin Valley, the River Alwin your constant companion.

> The River Alwin joins the River Coquet to the south of Alwinton. Grey Heron can often be seen fishing these waters. They are Britain's largest long-legged bird with a length of 90 to 98 cm. Grey and Pied Wagtail also frequent these waters. The Pied Wagtail is the only black and white

bird found throughout all seasons in Britain. The Grey Wagtail can be distinguished from the Pied by its yellow underside.

At the foot of the valley the buildings of Clennell appear. As you approach the farm buildings leave the main track and take the minor track leading off half-left. Walk down this track with a stone wall to your right until you reach a gate, pass through the gate. There is a house to your left here. Continue along the track on a tree lined avenue.

The caravans seen to your right belong to Clennell caravan Site, a mixture of static and mobile units. There are also log cabins and these are available to rent from the site. In the main building bed and breakfast accommodation is available and a bar which serves food. Walkers are also welcome here.

At a gate at the end of the track, pass through and turn right along the side of a stone wall a dozen or so paces to reach a gate. Go through the gate and a surfaced track guides you left, through the caravans with a wood also to your left. Remain on the track to reach a surfaced road where you turn right. Continue on the road to reach a metal bridge spanning the River Alwin running on your left. Cross the bridge and follow a path up the slope. Remain on the path as it crosses over two fields to reach a stone track (Clennell Street). Turn left and follow the track to return to your starting point.

33. Alwinton to Shillmoor

A walk using an old highway outwards and an old 'guard' road on the return.

Distance: 13km (8 miles)

Grade: Moderate

Maps: Ordnance Survey Landranger 80. Pathfinders 487 NT81/91 and 499 NT80/90. Outdoor Leisure 16.

Start: Alwinton car park. GR919063.

Proceed as in 'Alwinton to Kidlandlee' until you reach the ruins of Wholehope.

Pass to the left of the ruins of Wholehope and continue to reach a gate leading into a large coniferous plantation. Pass through the gate and proceed along a grassy path to meet a broad forestry road. Turn left and follow this road through the trees exiting via a further gate on the border of the plantation. Walk parallel to the plantation on your right on the rough road for 150 metres to reach a wooden marker post to the left of the road.

The marker post bear a blue arrow pointing ahead and a yellow arrow pointing left marked permissive path.

Turn left as indicated by the yellow arrow and, leaving the route of Clennell Street, follow a grassy path which leads you to the corner of the plantation to your left. At the corner a yellow arrow directs you to turn right, the path continuing parallel to a wire fence on your left. Keep to the path until you reach a gate in this fence. There is a stone sheep fold on your right. Cross the fence using a stile to the right of the gate. Keeping half-right, as indicated by a yellow arrow on the stile, follow a broad grassy path which leads you up a slope to the top of the hill ahead.

The deep valley to your right is that of the Usway Burn. This is one of the most exposed stretches of the walk and quite high winds are possible. My last trip over this section was in winter and the strength of the wind was unbelievable. I think I crawled sideways for most of the time.

After crossing the top of the hill the path descends to meet up with a broad stone track. There is a wooden marker post here. Turn right and follow the

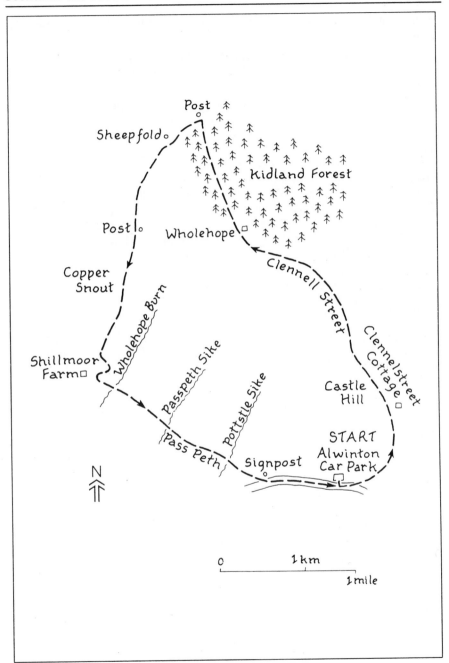

Post

Sheepfold

Kidland Forest

Post

Wholehope

Clennell Street

Copper Snout

Wholehope Burn

Clennelstreet Cottage

Shillmoor Farm

Passpeth Sike

Pottstle Sike

Castle Hill

Pass Peth

Signpost

START Alwinton Car Park

N

0   1 km

1 mile

track as it descends a short distance before climbing a low hill to reach a wire fence.

The view ahead overlooks part of the Otterburn Training Range. British and NATO forces come here to practice firing of weapons and NATO airforces practice air-to- ground attacks.

Pass through the gate in the fence and continue descending the track. Soon the buildings of Shillmoor farm appear ahead. Just before reaching the buildings the track bends left passing to the right of a sheep fold and a brick built hut. The track then bends to the right and descends to meet a stone wall. Turn left and walk parallel with the wall on your right heading away from Shillmoor. At a wire fence cross via the stile to the left of the gate and immediately ford the Wholehope Burn. From here the path runs parallel to the River Coquet to arrive at a further wire fence. Cross using the stile and walk on fording Passpeth Sike. Once across the sike the path forks. Take the left fork and follow the path as it climbs steeply up the side of the hill. At the top keep to the path as it crosses two farm tracks to reach a wire fence.

This path is historically known as Pass Peth. During the troubled times of Border warfare in the 15th and 16th century two local men were assigned to patrol this stretch day and night ready to sound the alarm if they sighted any raiding parties coming over from Scotland.

Cross the wire fence via a stile to the side of the gate. The path continues parallel to a wire fence on your left, gently descending to arrive at another fence. Pass through the gate and walk on, fording Pottstile Sike ahead. The path then descends to a gate leading to a surfaced road. To the side of the gate is a signpost 'Public bridleway to Shillmoor'. Pass through the gate and turn left to follow the road for 1.5km to return to Alwinton and the start of the walk.

34. Alwinton Valley Circular

A pleasant walk around a beautiful valley.

Distance: 7.5km (4½ miles)

Grade: Easy

Maps: Ordnance Survey Landranger 80. Ordnance Survey Pathfinder 499 NT80/90. Ordnance Survey Outdoor Leisure 16.

Start: Alwinton car park, GR919063.

Leave the car park and turn left to pass the house on the village street. Where the road bends to the right continue straight ahead towards the wooden bridge spanning the burn. Cross the bridge and turn left along a surfaced road which soon peters out to become a stone track. The track rises to reach a gate set in a stone wall. Pass through the gate and continue upwards passing to the left of the cottage known as Clennellstreet.

This track you are on is known as Clennell Street. It is very old and has been in use since pre Roman times. Over the centuries it has been used by travellers, traders, smugglers and the movement of livestock across the border between Scotland and England.

After passing the cottage the path forks. There is a wooden marker post here. Take the right-hand fork which climbs a short slope to reach a gate in a wire fence. Pass through the gate and then turn half-left to walk a dozen or so paces to reach another fence. This time cross using the stile provided. Follow a grassy path which contours high above the valley dropping away to your right.

This is the valley of the River Alwin along which you will be making your return trip. Alwin is an old word meaning clear or white water.

At a fork in the path take the right-hand fork and continue to reach a wire fence. Pass through a gap in the fence and walk on to reach another fork in the path, again favouring the right fork. A broad track takes you down to the floor of the valley. At a gate at the foot of the descent pass through and on to a broad roughly surfaced track.

A signpost to the left of the gate bears directions to Alwinton 2½ miles. The large plantation to your left is Kidland, one of the larger plantations within the Cheviots.

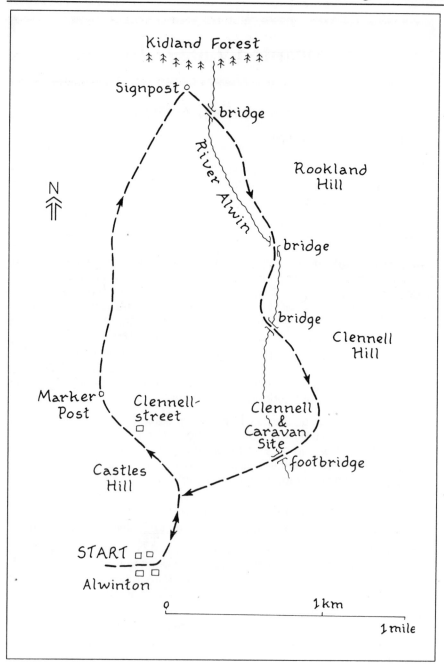

Kidland Forest

Signpost

bridge

River Alwin

Rookland Hill

bridge

bridge

Clennell Hill

N

Marker Post

Clennell-street

Clennell & Caravan Site

footbridge

Castles Hill

START

Alwinton

0   1 km

1 mile

Turn right to follow the rough track which will then lead you down the length of the valley criss-crossing the river on its meanderings.

Take a gentle stroll down this valley and soak in the wonderful scenery. Watch the fish darting in the river, scuttling to hide when the shadow of a heron passes over. On the level land near the river traces of mole, water vole and shrew can be detected. There are ample resting places besides the river for children.

At the foot of the valley the buildings of Clennell appear. Just before them take the minor track leading off half-left to skirt around the left of the buildings.

Clennell is the family seat of the Clennell family who have occupied the land as far back as the 13th century during the reign of King Edward I.

At a gate across the track pass through, there is a house to your left here. Continue to the next gate and pass through then turn right to walk parallel to a stone wall for a dozen paces to reach a gate in the wall. Pass through and into Clennell Caravan Site.

The main building of the site has a bar which serves meals, walkers are welcome here. Bed and breakfast accommodation is also available.

A surfaced track leads you left through the caravans with a wood to your left. Remain on the track to reach a surfaced road. Turn right at the road and continue until you reach a bridge spanning the River Alwin flowing on your left. Cross over the bridge and up the slope following a waymarked path. Continue over two fields, via gates, to reach a stone track (Clennell Street again). Turn left and follow the track to return to your start with memories of a short pleasant walk.

35. Alwinton to Batailshiel Haugh and Clennell Street

Travel up a delightful valley and return along an old cross-border smuggling route.

Distance: 23km (14 miles)

Grade: Moderate, but long.

Maps: Ordnance Survey Landranger 80. Pathfinders 487 NT81/91 and 499 NT80/90. Outdoor Leisure 16.

Start: Alwinton Car Park. GR919063.

On leaving the car park turn right and follow the surfaced road for 1.5km to reach a gate in the wire fence to your right. By the side is a signpost for Shillmoor. Pass through the gate and follow a grassy path which climbs a slope to reach a wire fence. Cross via the stile and continue on this path with a wire fence to your right to reach another wire fence crossing your path. Once again cross using a stile. Remain on this path as it crosses two farm tracks before descending steeply to the Passpeth Sike.

Back in the days of Border strife and fighting two men were always on patrol along this stretch to give warning if any marauding parties were sighted approaching from Scotland. Alwinton was frequently attacked during these times and local farms were often plundered for sheep and cattle.

Ford the sike and walk on with the River Coquet to your left to arrive at the Wholehope Burn. Ford the burn and climb the stile set in the fence immediately after the burn. The path now runs parallel to the stone wall on your left. Ahead can be seen the farm buildings of Shillmoor. When the wall ends continue straight ahead to a concrete bridge spanning the Usway Burn. Cross the bridge and aim for a gate to the left of the large barn ahead until. Pass through the gate and along the surfaced road to the left of the farm buildings until you come to a large sign board to the right of the road.

This bears the notice 'Ministry of Defence. Private road. No vehicles will be taken beyond this point except by authorised persons'.

Turn sharp right here to leave the road and proceed along a stony track which

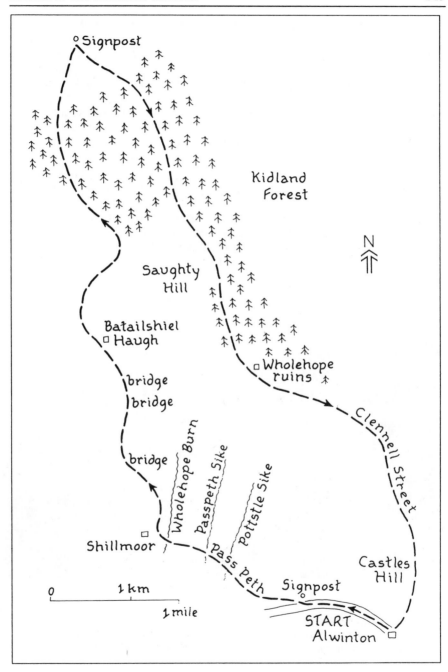

Signpost

Kidland
Forest

N

Saughty
Hill

Batailshiel
Haugh

bridge
bridge

Wholehope
ruins

Clennell Street

bridge

Wholehope Burn

Passpeth Sike

Pottstle Sike

Shillmoor

Pass Peth

Signpost

Castles
Hill

0   1 km

1 mile

START
Alwinton

rises and curves to the left crossing a cattle grid. Remain on the track as it takes you up the valley with the Usway Burn flowing to your right. Pass to the left of a sheep fold and across another cattle grid. Cross a dark-green bridge across the burn. Still further up the valley another two similar bridges also have to be crossed. After crossing the last bridge the track curves left and the buildings of Batailshiel Haugh can be seen ahead. Pass by a sign reading 'Out of bounds to military traffic' and on to cross a cattle grid. At the stone wall surrounding Batailshiel Haugh do not pass through the gate. Turn right to follow a permissive path which takes you around the perimeter of the farm.

The word 'shiel' as in Batailshiel means summer pastures. In Medieval times it was common practice for shepherds to graze their sheep on the higher hills during the summer and then move them down to lower land when winter came. Shiels were temporary structures built by the shepherds for the summer months. Generally they were stone built with two rooms and a turf covered roof. The ruins of many of these shiels can be still be found today throughout the area.

Batailshiel farm

After passing the farm, ford a narrow burn and climb the bank following a grassy path. Keep a wire fence to your left until you reach a marker post bearing a blue arrow to the side of the path. Turn left as indicated by the arrow and descend a dip to ford the burn at the bottom. Climb out of the dip and continue along the path with the Usway Burn to your left. Pass to the right of a sheep fold and continue on to cross a small burn at the corner of a plantation. The path bends left here passing to the left of a sheep fold before reaching a fence across the path. Cross using the stile and continue along the path as it passes through trees keeping the Usway Burn to your left. After 1km the path arrives at the cottage of Fairhaugh. Pass to the left of the cottage and cross the wooden foot bridge spanning the Usway Burn.

This is an idyllic spot to rest and relax.

After crossing the bridge turn half-left for a dozen or so paces across a grassy slope to reach a forestry road. Turn right at the road and follow it as it climbs through the trees, later descending to a gate which allows you to exit from the plantation. From the gate a farm track leads you on a dozen paces to reach a wooden marker post. Turn right as indicated by the blue arrow following a grassy path which takes you along the side of Hazely Law to reach a wire fence. Cross via the stile provided continuing on a track for 65m to reach a stile set in a wire fence to your right. Cross over the stile.

You are now on Clennell Street. This was an old trading route stretching 19km from Alwinton to Hownam in Scotland. It was used by pedlars, drovers, reivers and smugglers. Its heyday was during the 18th and 19th centuries when around 100,000 cattle a year would be driven across the border.

The path descends to a footbridge which spans the Usway Burn. Cross the burn and follow the path which rises to the right leading to a plantation. On entering the trees keep to the path to reach a forestry road. Turn left on this forestry road through the trees for 1km to reach a gate allowing you to leave the plantation. The track continues beside the trees with open ground to your right soon reaching a further gate which takes you back into the plantation. Follow the forestry road for about 1km and where the road bends to the left continue ahead down a path to reach a gate which allows you to leave the plantation yet again. After passing through the gate follow a broad track to another gate. Pass through this.

If you look left you will notice the ruins of Wholehope. Originally a shepherd's house it later became a Youth Hostel. But due to its isolation it was later closed and has been left to decay.

Pass by the ruins and remain on the grassy track as it descends a slope to reach a gate in a wire fence. Pass through and follow the track with the plantation to your left. Soon the plantation curves away to your left and you cross open ground to reach a gate in a wire fence. Pass through the gate and continue with sheep pens to your right. After passing the pens the track descends slightly to pass through a gate before rising to climb the side of a hill. The track contours the side of the hill, with a wire fence to your left. After

1km the track descends to reach a wooden marker post to the left of the track. Pass by the post and walk on keeping the stone wall to your left. Behind the wall lies the cottage of Clennellstreet.

Just past Clennellstreet to your right is Castles Hill. On its summit are the remains of an Iron Age fort and settlement.

At a metal gate across the track pass through and continue descending as the track takes you to Alwinton. You reach a wooden foot bridge spanning the Hoseden Burn on your right. Cross the bridge and proceed over the village green and along the village street to pass to the right of the Rose and Thistle Inn to return to the car park and the start of this walk.

36. Barrowburn to Davison's Linn

This begins with a gentle uphill walk and then goes on to visit a delightful waterfall in a quiet valley.

Distance: 12km (7½ miles)

Grade: Easy/Moderate

Maps: Ordnance Survey Landranger 80. Ordnance Survey Pathfinder 487 NT81/91. Ordnance Survey Outdoor Leisure 16.

Start: Wedder Leap car park (GR866103) near Barrowburn farm in the Coquet Valley.

Overnight camping is permitted at Davison's Linn. A permit is required and this can be obtained by getting in touch with Forest Enterprises, 1 Walley Hill, Rothbury, Northumberland NE65 7NT, or telephone Rothbury (01669) 620569. Permits are free.

On leaving the car park turn left and walk down the surfaced road until you reach a wooden foot bridge to your right spanning the River Coquet. Cross the bridge then cross the stile to your right. After a few steps cross a further stile to your left. Continue over a grass field with trees on your left. At a wire fence pass through the gate and walk parallel to a stone wall. At a fence running across the path cross again using a stile and continue until you are adjacent to a group of buildings to your left, this was Windyhaugh School. Here another stile in the fence to your left leads on after a few paces to reach a broad track.

The former school building has been converted to a camping barn for school parties and walking groups. The school itself was opened in 1878 and the first schoolmaster was a Mr Blythe who originated from Yetholm. Mr Blythe only had the use of one hand and pupils had to assist him each day in the filling of his pipe. Over the years a decline in the number of pupils led to the school being closed in 1978.

Turn right on to the track and walk on to reach a gate. Pass through the gate and follow the track which rises and contours around the side of Kyloe Shin before dropping towards the floor of the valley. The track travels over a short stretch of level ground before rising steeply up the side of Kyloe Shin again.

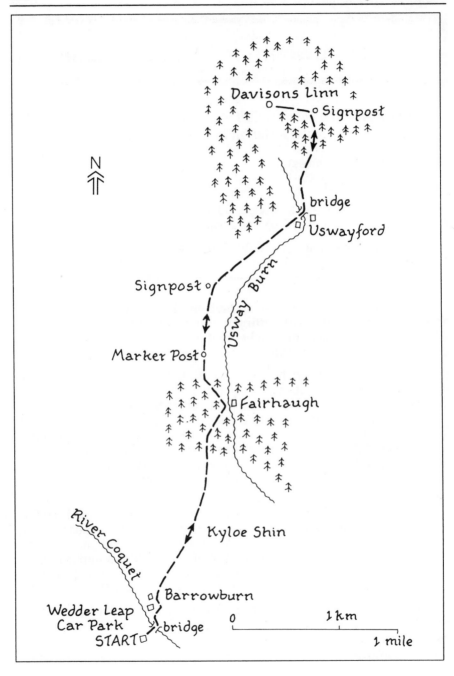

N

Davisons Linn
o Signpost

bridge
Uswayford

Usway Burn

Signpost o

Marker Post o

Fairhaugh

Kyloe Shin

River Coquet

Barrowburn

Wedder Leap
Car Park
START
bridge

0   1 km

1 mile

At the top, continue; there is a deep valley to your left. The track soon brings you to a gate leading into a coniferous plantation.

Coniferous plantations within the Cheviots usually comprise of one or more of four species of tree, the Sitka Spruce, the Norway Spruce, the Scots Pine and the Larch. All of these are ideally suited for the area with their ability to establish themselves easily and survive the often harsh winter conditions.

Once into the plantation follow the broad track leading through the trees until you reach a wooden marker post. Continue ahead as indicated by a blue arrow, the track descending to the banks of the Usway Burn. The cottage of Fairhaugh is visible to the other side of the burn. Where the track bends right towards the cottage leave the track and turn left on to a grassy path. There is a marker post here with a blue arrow.

The wooden bridge to your right leads to Fairhaugh. Sheltered by trees this is an idyllic place to rest and have a bite to eat by the burn. Brown trout dart to and fro and the burn gives musical entertainment as it tumbles over the falls to your left.

A grassy path climbs up through the trees. Passing a marker post and ignoring a turning to the left continue as the path makes a gentle descent to a gate. Cross over the stile next to the gate and exit from the plantation. A good farm track leads you on a dozen paces to reach a marker post. Leave the track here and follow a grassy path as indicated by the blue arrow on the marker post. The path leads you by the side of Hazely Law to reach a wire fence. Cross via the stile and on to a track for 100m to reach a four finger signpost.

This signpost bears directions for Clennell Street, Uswayford, Trows, Rowhope and the Border ridge. Looking to the right you can catch a glimpse of the buildings of Uswayford set amidst a cluster of trees.

Turn right to follow the track in the direction of Uswayford contouring the side of Ward Law to reach a fork in the track. Take the right-hand fork and pass through a metal gate. A stone track leads you towards Uswayford. After passing to the left of a large barn the track bends right to descend towards the farm house. Turn left at the bend leaving the track to follow a grassy path leading to a wooden foot bridge spanning the Usway Burn.

The farm at Uswayford has the somewhat dubious distinction of being one of remotest farms in England. In the days before motor transport pedlars bought goods ordered by the shepherd's family up as far as Barrowburn. The shepherd met the pedlars to collect his goods, no doubt exchanging news and gossip along with the groceries.

After crossing the bridge turn left and cross a fence. A narrow path takes you along the side of Hen Hill before descending to the valley floor. Ford a small burn crossing the path then climb a rise in front ahead. At a wire fence at the top of the slope cross, using the stile, and continue parallel to a wire fence on your right. The path later veers left away from the fence and leads into a plantation. Continue through the trees to reach a signpost bearing directions for Salters Road East and West. Take the left-hand path as indicated Salters Road West and pass through trees before emerging into a clearing above a valley. The path bends right descending to reach a signpost. Turn left at the signpost and down a slope to cross a burn. The noise of the waterfall announces you have arrived at Davison's Linn.

If you are camping here for the night please clear your site and remove all litter before you depart. Those continuing on to Windy Gyle should turn to the respective pages.

37. Barrowburn to Windy Gyle

A leg-stretching walk to visit one of the higher summits in the Cheviots with a spectacular view into Scotland.

Distance: 15km (9 miles)

Grade: Strenuous

Maps: Ordnance Survey Landranger 80. Ordnance Survey Pathfinder 487 NT81/91. Ordnance Survey Outdoor Leisure 16.

Start: Wedder Leap car park (GR866103) near Barrowburn Farm in the Coquet Valley.

Proceed as in the walk 'Barrowburn to Davison's Linn' until you reach Davison's Linn.

After crossing the burn climb the short steep rise ahead until. A path leads on through a coniferous plantation. At a forest road cross and continue through trees to reach a wire fence. Cross via a stile next to the gate.

Davison's Linn

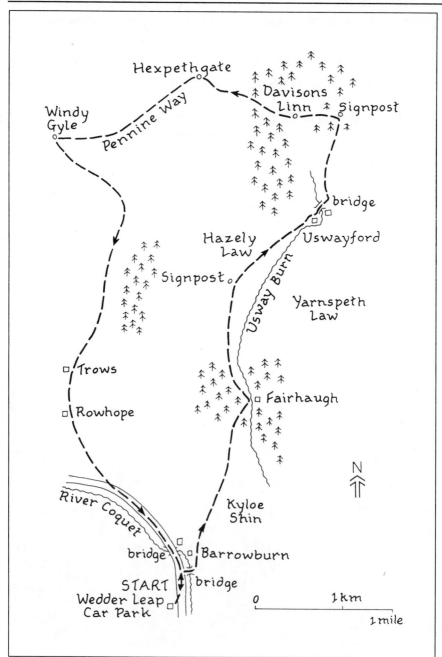

A signpost at the gate bears directions for Uswayford and Salters Road East and Salters Road West. Salters Road is an old drove road.

Walk straight ahead to reach another signpost. This one bears directions for Clennell Street, Uswayford, Low Bleakhope and Alwinton. Turn right following the directions for Clennell Street over a rough track which rises to a wire fence with gates and a four finger signpost.

This is Hexpethgate, an ancient Border crossing point. In the 15th and 16th century when the Border was in a state of turmoil and bloodshed this was a neutral meeting place where the Lords Wardens of the Marches, who attempted to keep some sort of law and order, met and talked to try and sort out local rights and wrongs.

Turn left and follow a well-trodden path which is part of the Pennine Way. At a fence across the way cross via the stile and continue as the path rises towards the summit of Windy Gyle.

Due to the large number of walkers travelling along the Pennine Way the peaty surface has eroded badly. To combat the erosion parts of the Pennine Way have been paved with large mill stones laid by the National Park.

At the summit of Windy Gyle pass through a gate in the fence to your right and proceed towards the distinctive summit cairn, topped with an Ordnance Survey triangulation column.

The view from the summit is quite stunning, a 360 degree panorama stretching deep into England and Scotland making this walk well worth it. On the summit stands a white stone Ordnance Survey column. The first mappings by Ordnance Survey were carried out in 1791 when the army required accurate mapping of the south coast because of a possible invasion from France. Ordnance Survey came into being during the Industrial Revolution mapping out new roads and towns. Now a government department, the Ordnance Survey produce a vast array of maps. In the early days maps were produced by surveyors on foot walking the land using chains and tapes. Today satellite observations and computer technology have greatly improved the service and made map making easier.

Retrace your steps back to the gate and pass through. Continue straight ahead following a descending path amply supplied with marker posts to guide you on your way. As you descend a plantation soon becomes visible to your left whilst to your right the ground drops away to a deep valley. The path continues to descend, soon dropping quite steeply to reach the farm house at Trows. Just before the house is a wide burn which is crossed via a wooden foot bridge.

It is recommended that this foot bridge be used. My wife, in attempting to cross the burn by the ford, slid on the slippery stones and collapsed in a comical heap only to spend the rest of the walk in wet trousers.

Pass to the left of the farm house (at present empty – 1996) then continue along a surfaced road with the Rowhope Burn to your side. Soon you pass the farm at Rowhope. Remain on the surfaced road down the valley. At a cattle grid cross on to a surfaced motor road turning left to return to your starting point. The River Coquet accompanies you along this stretch.

Wedder Leap has an interesting story behind its name. During the troubled times of Border strife, a thief by the name of Wedder who had stolen a sheep, which in those days was known as a 'wedder', was being pursued and reached the banks of the Coquet. Rather than risk capture, he leaped across the gap, a distance of nearly 5 metres. One version of the story tells that he successfully jumped and reached the other side to escape. Another tells that he jumped and just reached the bank but the weight of the sheep tied on his back pulled him backwards and into the river where he drowned.

38. Barrowburn to Windy Gyle via The Street

An easy climb up to one of the highest peaks in the area.

Distance: 17km (10½ miles)

Grade: Moderate

Maps: Ordnance Survey Landranger 80. Pathfinder 487 NT81/91. Outdoor Leisure 16.

Start: Wedder Leap car park. GR866103.

On leaving the parking area turn left and follow the surfaced road, passing the buildings of Barrowburn before crossing the road bridge over the River Coquet. Keeping the Coquet on your left follow the road for just under a kilometre to reach a bridge spanning the Rowhope Burn. Cross the bridge before passing through the gate in the wire fence to your right.

You are now at the start of The Street. This was an old drovers and trade route across the Border. Used in bygone days it linked Alwinton with Hownam in Scotland. It dates from pre-Roman times and is named Clattering Path on old maps.

After passing through the gate follow the path as it climbs the slopes of a hill with a wire fence to your left. Where the fence bends half-right turn with it and continue parallel with the fence for 250 metres to reach a stile set in it.

As you climb the view to the right overlooks the Rowhope Valley. Below are the buildings of Rowhope farm and further up the valley eastwards can be seen the farm at Trows. Above and slightly to the left of Trows rises the summit of Windy Gyle.

Cross via the stile and continue climbing towards the summit of Swinehope Law keeping the fence to your right. As you gain height the path bends slightly to the right thus by-passing the actual summit. The path then makes a short descent before climbing again to climb the slope of Black Braes. At the top continue to reach a wire fence and a well-used path.

The fence is the Border fence separating England and Scotland. The path is part of the Pennine Way, a long distance footpath stretching from Edale in Derbyshire to Kirk Yetholm in Scotland.

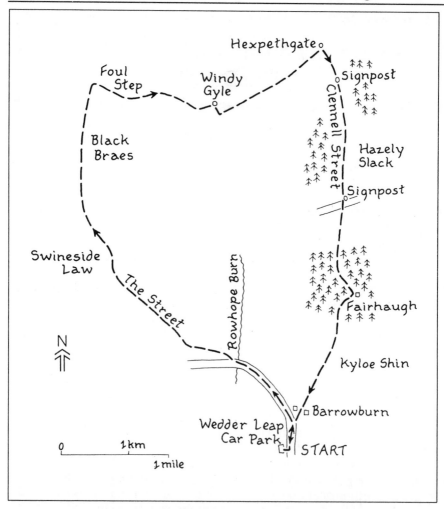

Continue, keeping the Border fence on your left until before a gate across the way you reach a path leading off to the right. Turn right to join this path thus leaving The Street and walk over rough grassland to reach a small shallow valley. Descend into the valley crossing the burn at its foot before climbing out again.

This is Foul Step, aptly named if crossed after a spell of wet weather.

The path contours above a deep valley to your right. At a wire fence, your old friend the Border fence again, turn right and keeping adjacent to the fence commence your ascent of Windy Gyle. Soon you reach a stile set in the fence. Cross here and turn right. The path continues climbing across the rough grass. Follow a path branching left to reach the distinctive summit of Windy Gyle.

Windy Gyle at 619 metres is one of the higher peaks in the Cheviots. A unique feature of Windy Gyle is the large cairn on the summit. This was a Bronze Age burial mound but in recent times has become known as Russells Cairn in memory of Lord Francis Russell who was fatally shot at a March Wardens meeting at nearby Hexpethgate,. It is thought that the actual cairn built to mark his murder was built below and to the right of the summit.

Walk south away from the cairn to reach a gate set in the Border fence. Pass through the gate and turn left to rejoin the Pennine Way as it descends towards a wire fence across the way. Pass through the gate in this fence and continue on keeping the Border fence to your left for about 2km to reach a gate in the fence and a four finger signpost.

This is Hexpethgate, a neutral meeting place during the years of Border strife in the 15th and 16th centuries where the March Wardens held meetings to sort out local disputes. It was here Lord Francis Russell was murdered in the summer of 1585.

Take the path marked for "Clennell Street, Alwinton, Uswayford" descending a broad grassy path to reach a further signpost. Continue ahead following the Clennell Street marker on this post until you encounter a wire fence crossing the path. Pass through a gate in this fence and continue ahead, there is a plantation visible to your left. Remain on the path for 2km when it then descends Hazely Slack, with a plantation to your right, to arrive at a further four finger signpost.

Clennell Street is another of the ancient trade routes that were used for cross Border trade.

Cross over the rough farm road and following a track for 100 metres reach a wire fence across the way. Cross the fence using the stile provided to follow a grassy path taking you along the side of Hazely Law. At a wooden marker post bearing a blue arrow turn left as indicated down a farm track to reach a gate leading into a large coniferous plantation. Cross the stile next to the gate and continue on an climbing path through trees. At the top of the rise the path forks. Take the left fork descending towards the banks of the Usway Burn.

This is one of my favourite spots in the Cheviots. Sitting by the banks of the burn and watching the trout play is an ideal way to relax. Sandpipers can often be seen along the banks feeding on small water insects. This small bird has a habit of bobbing its head up and down when at rest, a trait similar to that of the dipper bird. Close to the bank of the burn freshwater shrimps can be seen swimming about. These crustaceans have laterally compressed bodies which enable them to seek refuge under stones when danger threatens.

The path then bends right climbing through the trees to arrive at a gate which allows you to exit from the plantation. A broad path travels across the top of Kyloe Shin before descending steeply to the floor of the valley on your right. It then re-climbs contouring the lower reaches of Kyloe Shin before descending again to reach a gate leading to the farm buildings at Barrowburn. Pass through this gate and follow the track through Barrowburn to reach a surfaced road. Turn left at the road and follow it to return to your starting point.

On passing through Barrowburn notice the first building to your right, this has been converted to a camping barn for school parties and walking groups.

The cairn on the summit of Windy Gyle

39. Blindburn to Yearning Law

A charming valley walk up to the Border ridge and excellent views on the return.

Distance: 7.2km (4½ miles)

Grade: Moderate

Maps: Ordnance Survey Landranger 80. Ordnance Survey Pathfinder 499 NT80/90. Ordnance Survey Outdoor Leisure 16.

Start: At the car park at Buckams Walls Bridge GR830109.

Walk back to the signpost at the entrance to the car park. This bears directions for the Border ridge and Deels Hill. To the right of the signpost is a gate. Pass through this gate and on to a grassy path which leads up the valley. To your left flows the Buckham Walls Burn. About one kilometre up the valley ford a small burn which comes in from a valley to your right. Continue up the valley for another kilometre to reach a point where a valley comes in from your left across the burn. Two sheep folds are sited at the mouth of this valley.

Here, you will notice numerous hollows and ridges in the ground. These mark the site of an old medieval homestead. Remains like these are fairly common throughout the southern Cheviots. Generally they are of medieval origin but some can date back earlier to prehistoric times. The medieval ruins for the main part were homesteads belonging to the monks of Newminster Abbey who from 1181 to the dissolution of the monasteries in 1536 grazed sheep on these lands. Newminster Abbey is located near Morpeth and was built in 1157 only to be destroyed by raiding Scots in the same year. It was then rebuilt and became the largest Cistercian abbey in northern England.

Continue up the valley on a narrow path to pass to the left of a stone sheep fold. Then, after some 600m from this point, you encounter another sheep fold. Pass to the right of this and up a short steep slope, the top of which is covered with the hollows and ridges which again indicate the site of an old homestead.

This is also the site of a medieval homestead. In all probability also dating back to the time of the monks of Newminster Abbey. This area

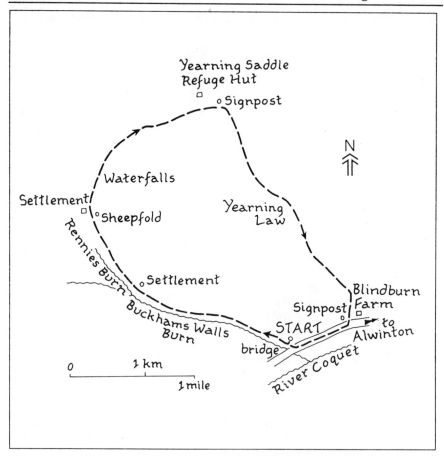

was also used as a hunting ground and, because of this, the monks had
to remove three claws from their dogs' forepaws to prevent them chasing
after the game.

After passing through the homestead, bear right and climb a slight slope.
Continue along a grassy path which takes you up a wide valley. Below to
your right flows a narrow burn.

Further upstream a series of pretty waterfalls is passed, well worth a
brief diversion for a closer look.

Some 400m after the waterfalls you will notice a narrow burn flowing down
the slope to your right and feeding into the burn you have followed. At the
point where they untie cross over and keep this smaller burn to your right as
you follow a grassy path up a slight slope to reach a wooden marker post.

Looking left here, the refuge hut of Yearning Saddle can be seen on the ridge. This provides a refuge for walkers undertaking the Pennine Way which follows along the top of the ridge.

Continue past the marker post to the next one visible on the rise ahead. At this post another is visible ahead. After this next post the path bends in a gentle curve to the right. Further marker posts guide you along and keep you on the correct path. Finally you will reach a marker post which bears directions for Yearning Law, Border Ridge and Rennies Burn (the direction you have just come). Continue straight ahead as indicated by the marker for Yearning Law on a broad grass path. A dozen steps later reaching a path branching off to the right. Turn on to this path and follow it through bracken to pass between the two distinctive humps marking the summit of Yearning Law.

It's well worth pausing on the top to admire the view with the hills rolling off in all directions and appreciate the silence. However on some days the silence is broken by loud bangs and crumps from guns firing at Otterburn to the south. Do not be alarmed at the noise, the army are not shooting at you but at each other.

Descend the other side to again reach a broad green path. This could be churned up in places due to tanks or heavy vehicles using the area from their base at nearby Otterburn. As you descend, it's not long before the buildings of Blindburn farm appear at the head of the valley to your left. The path descends to the buildings and passes to the side of them to reach a tarmac surfaced road. Turn right along the road to return to your starting point.

To your left flows the River Coquet. Many species of bird can be found along its banks including Wheatear, Grey Wagtail, Dipper, Goosander and Oyster Catcher. You may also be lucky to see a Grey Heron cruising past.

40. Blindburn to the Border Ridge

A stimulating walk up to and along the Border ridge.

Distance: 12km (7½ miles)

Grade: Moderate

Maps: Ordnance Survey Landranger 80. Pathfinders 486 NT61/71, 487 NT81/91 and 498 NT60/70. Outdoor Leisure 16.

Start: Car park at Buckhams Burn bridge. GR830109.

Leave the car park turning left to walk back down the surfaced road to the farm at Blindburn. Proceeding past the farm buildings and just before the bridge spanning the Blind Burn there is a signpost to the left of the road. This bears directions for Yearning Hall and the Border Ridge. Cross the wooden fence via the stile and follow a grassy path down the side of the farm. This takes you to a wire fence which you cross via the stile provided. Continue on a dozen metres to a second fence again crossing via a stile. Follow the path keeping the Blind Burn to your right. After about 270 metres you will come to a plank bridge spanning the burn. Cross this little bridge and then bear left to continue your walk up the valley.

> Wading birds are seen near the rivers and wider burns of the area. The oystercatcher is the most common and also the Common Sandpiper. Wild fowl such as the Gooseander can be found at the sides of the burn hunting for small fish. Lucky walkers may catch sight of the heron. There is no mistaking this large bird with its long legs. They are a delight to watch swooping along the water on the look out for the unwary fish or standing motionless at the water side.

At a fence across the path, cross via the stile. After about 50 metres cross the next fence using a stile to the right of the gate. A yellow arrow on the stile points your way ahead. The path continues up the valley following the right bank of the Blind Burn. Keeping left of a circular stone sheep fold in your path you will see a wooden marker post bearing a yellow arrow directing you ahead. Cross over a small sike utilising a wooden plank laid for the purpose and walk on to the next marker post you can see ahead until. Continue up the valley following the bank of the burn. Ignore any paths or tracks you may notice leading off to your right.

At a point where the valley divides look upwards towards the hilly skyline to your left where you will see the ruins of a cottage. This is the marker for your route.

Turn left and cross the Blind Burn, it is quite narrow here. A path takes you up a rise towards the old cottage. Just before the ruins the path drops into a narrow gully with a small sike at the bottom before climbing out steeply up the other side. Follow the path as it skirts firstly to the left of the ruins and then right towards what was once a gate in a fence. Most of the fence has now gone only the posts remain.

The ruins are those of Yearning Hall, which despite its grandiose title, is only a shepherd's cottage.

Yearning Hall

Pass through the gate posts and head towards a wooden marker post on the summit of the rise ahead. At the post continue straight ahead over a grassy path which rises gently ahead until. At the top of the rise and straight ahead until can be seen the squat, square-shaped refuge hut on Yearning Saddle, your next target. Remain on the grassy path to reach a marker post just before the hut. Turn left at this post.

If you want a break, walk straight ahead over the last few metres to reach the refuge hut. This provides shelter on a windy or cold day and is an

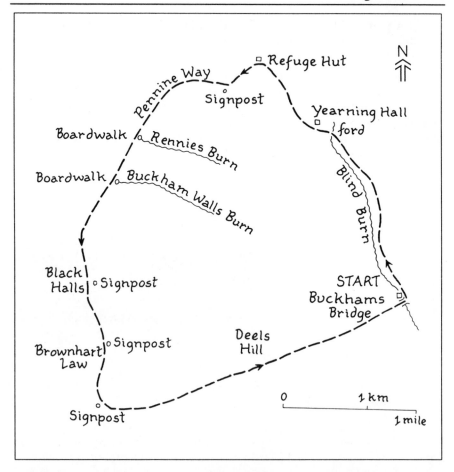

ideal spot for a refreshment break. The hut also provides a free overnight
shelter for walkers. Inside are three wooden benches, just wide enough
to sleep on.

Follow a well-trodden path, which is part of the Pennine Way, to climb a slight
rise to reach a signpost attached to a wire fence.

This fence is the Border fence denoting the border between Scotland
and England. Looking over the fence here, the view into Scotland is
seemingly infinite.

After passing the signpost the path angles left and away from the Border
fence. As you travel down the path you will pass a wooden marker post
bearing a blue arrow which helps to keep you on the right path although the

path here is very distinct. You will soon reach a narrow cleft which must be crossed. Climbing out of the cleft you will encounter another marker post directing you straight ahead.

This cleft is hard to cross after snow I had to make a large detour to accomplish this last winter, so be prepared for a detour if attempting this bit in winter.

About a dozen metres on the path curves to the left and after passing the next marker post and 90 metres onwards you come across a short stretch of wooden duckboards.

These boards enable you to cross the start of Rennies Burn without getting your feet wet or sinking into the mud.

Cross the duckboards and continue over bleak moor land guided by occasional marker posts. After passing a large stone cairn you will encounter another short stretch of wooden duckboards.

Thankfully another wet and boggy area avoided. This is the start of Buckhams Burn.

Once across the duckboards the path continues gradually climbing the slope of Brownhart Law to reach a marker post.

Looking right there is a magnificent view to the west overlooking Scotland. I was once up here and had the good fortune to see two wild goats on the other side of the fence. During the time of the Roman occupation of the area there was a signal station situated on the summit of Brownhart Law.

The path descends slightly to meet up with a second encounter with the Border fence. The path runs parallel and to the left of the fence, soon reaching a four finger signpost.

The signpost bears directions for the Pennine Way, Chew Green, Tow Ford and Blindburn.

Continue from the signpost keeping the Border fence to your right as you walk along an old Roman road known as Dere Street to reach another four finger signpost. Turn left here, following the directions for Deels Hill and Blindburn. The path, climbing gently, soon reaches the top of Deels Hill before descending towards a wire fence set with a gate. Cross the fence using a stile to the left of the gate and continue to a further fence across your path. This time pass through the gate to begin your final descent taking you though a metal gate leading into the car park and the culmination of your walk.

41. Biddlestone to Singmoor

A gentle walk into the lower Cheviot Hills

Distance: 5.5km (3½ miles)

Grade: Easy

Maps: Ordnance Survey Landranger 81. Ordnance Survey Pathfinder 499 NT80/90. Ordnance Survey Outdoor Leisure 16.

Start: Telephone box at Biddlestone GR961083.

Turn left (north) from your parking spot and take the first road to the right signposted 'Elilaw and Biddleston Town Foot'. Walk on for 100m to reach a gate in the fence to your left. Cross via the stile next to the fence and head over the field walking slightly to the left to reach a gate in the far left-hand corner of the field. Pass through the gate and turn left to immediately pass through another. Turn right on to a red stoned track and follow as it climbs Bleakmoor Hill.

> To your left is Harden Quarry. The red felspar obtained from the quarry was formed 300 million years ago. This is used to surface many of the roads and tracks within the southern Cheviots as well as used for road building nationwide. In London the Mall leading to Buckingham Palace is surfaced with red felspar obtained from this quarry. The quarry though unsightly and out of place in a National Park provides many local jobs in an area of little employment. A compromise must be made of necessity between local needs and the scenery within the Park.

Continue on the track passing through a gate until you reach a point before it dipping into a deep gully with a narrow burn at the bottom. Here, turn right and leave the track heading over rough grass to the fence visible on your right. At the fence turn left and walk parallel to it until you encounter a gate across the path. Pass through the gate and turn half-left as the path descends into the gully. At the lowest point ford Smawdon Sike. To your left are some sheep pens.

> In Northumberland, sheep folds are stone walled circular enclosures. They are used by shepherds for the gathering and sheltering of sheep, especially so in winter when the sheep could be fed in a safe place.

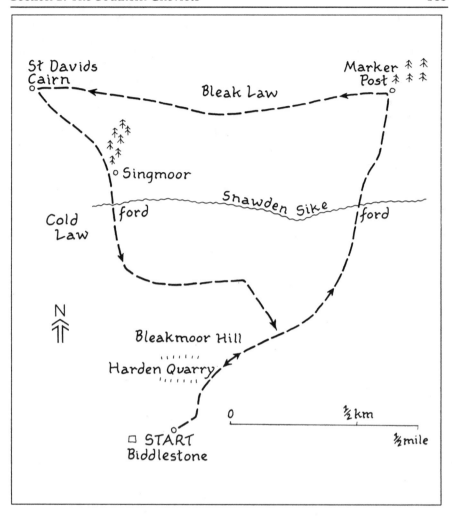

Nowadays they are not used so much and consequently a great number have fallen into disuse.

The path climbs out of the gully leading across heather moorland towards the left-hand corner of a plantation which becomes visible ahead. A few metres before the corner you will come upon a wooden marker post. Turn sharply left at the post to follow a grassy path which rises up a slope. When a plantation becomes visible ahead bear half-right to pass to the right of the trees. Some 300m to the right of the plantation wooden marker posts assist and guide you to the top of the slope.

Looking back on the ascent, you are rewarded with many really fine views of the Vale of Whittingham spread out below and the Simonside hills etched on the skyline. The sandstone rim of the Simonside Hills was formed 300 million years ago as large sandy deltas spread across the area. Much later folding and faulting of the land created the escarpments which are visible today.

Ignore the first broad track which crosses your path continuing straight ahead until you encounter a second track. This track will bear a wooden marker post with blue and yellow direction arrows set in a small cairn of stones.

On maps this is referred to as St Davids Cairn.

Walkers on the Gills Law walk should now turn to the relevant page and continue from this point.

Turn left at the post and along the track as it descends towards Singmoor soon passing to the right of a coniferous plantation and then reaching the cottage itself. The track passes to the right of the cottage and on to a gate. Pass through the gate and follow the track into a gully before it climbs again. Remain on the stone track, retracing your steps from the beginning of the walk, to return to your starting point.

42. Biddlestone Gills Law Circular

Another gentle walk exploring the lower Cheviot hills

Distance: 7.5km (4½ miles)

Grade: Easy

Maps: Ordnance Survey Landrangers 80 and 81. Ordnance Survey Pathfinders 499 NT80/90 and 487 NT81/91.

Start: At the telephone box at Biddlestone GR961083.

Proceed as in walk 'Biddlestone to Singmoor' to the marker post known as St Davids Cairn, next to a red stone track. Turn right at the cairn to reach a gate. Cross over the stile to the left of the gate and continue along a broad grassy path.

To your left is a deep valley with the Biddlestone Burn at the bottom.

The path soon dips to ford a burn before rising to pass left of a ruined sheep fold. About 25m on take a small grassy path which leads off left. This contours around the left side of Bleak Law. Descend over rough grass towards a ruined sheep fold. At a gate, pass through and ford the burn. The path rises to pass to the right of the sheep fold continuing onwards to reach a gate in a wire fence. Pass through and bear half-left to ford another burn before climbing the short steep rise ahead. At the top of the rise look half-left for a stile in a wire fence. On sighting it cross the moor towards it. Cross the stile and turn right to pass through a gate. Continue parallel to the fence on your right for 200m to reach a gate in the fence.

Below and in front are the buildings of Puncherton, a sheep stock farm. A shepherd's life in the Cheviots is often hard and lonely. The sheep season begins in November when the 'tups' (rams) are put in with the 'ewes' (sheep). During winter the snow covers the grazing land and the shepherd has to carry out bales of hay to the sheep no matter what the weather. Hill lambing begins around mid-April and this is the shepherd's busiest time. In July, the sheep are clipped of their coats and a month later they are dipped to eliminate any parasites or disease.

Here, turn left away from the fence and follow a path into a small valley. Ford the burn at the bottom and go up a path which takes you out of the valley. Descend a slight slope until you reach a red stoned farm track.

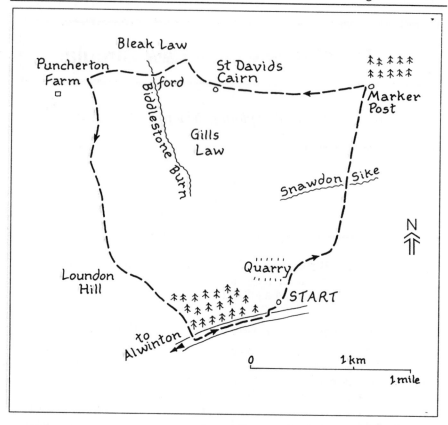

The red stone tracks encountered throughout this region of the Cheviots all have their origin from stones quarried at nearby Harden Quarry.

At the track turn left and follow it to reach a gate. Pass through it and walk on for 250m. Just after the bend you will see a grassy path leading off to your left. Leave the track and follow this path as it climbs Loundon Hill.

Looking back from the top of the hill, you can see the undulating line of Cheviot Hills along the horizon. Ahead is the familiar sight of the Simonside Hills. These are topped with a large desolate moor and an interesting folk tale tells of elves who live on the moor who delight in leading unwary travellers into the bogs or off the end of the crags.

Cross over the broad flat top of Loundon Hill and remain on the path as it descends to reach a plantation. The path runs parallel to the trees and descends to a metal gate. Pass through the gate and on a dozen paces to reach a red stone track. At the track turn left and follow it down through trees until you emerge on to a surfaced road. Turn left and follow this road to return to Biddlestone and the start of your walk. Biddlestone Cottage is on the right.

43. Biddlestone to Puncherton and Old Rookland

A gentle climb takes you on to the hills before visiting the ruins of an old farmstead.

Distance: 6.4km (4 miles)

Grade: Easy

Maps: Ordnance Survey Landrangers 80 and 81. Ordnance Survey Pathfinders 499 NT80/90 and 487 NT81/91. Ordnance Survey Outdoor Leisure 16.

Start: At the telephone box at Biddlestone GR961083.

Leave your parking spot and walk back a dozen paces (south) to the public road. Turn right along this road to reach a track on your right leading into a forest. Leave the road and a follow the track to pass through a gate. Walk on for 20m then turn right to leave the track and through a break in the trees. At first the way is indistinct and care should be taken to avoid partly hidden branches in the undergrowth. Persevere and after passing a hollow you will emerge on to a well-defined path. Turn left and follow it through the trees parallel to a deep valley on your right soon emerging into a clearing with Biddlestone Chapel on your left.

Roman Catholic Biddlestone Chapel is built on the ruins of an ancient pele tower. This tower is mentioned in the Border Surveys of 1541 and 1451. Biddlestone has always been the chief centre for Roman Catholics in Upper Coquetdale. The chapel today is empty and abandoned but in 1996 the building was in the process of being renovated.

Pass by the chapel turning right to pass the front entrance. Then turn half-left to reach a gap in the trees. Follow a narrow path through the trees. There is a deep ravine to your left at first but this soon angles away from you. Remain on this path until you emerge on to a broad track surfaced with red stones. Turn right along this track climbing as it rises to reach Biddlestone cottage. At the point where the track bends sharply left to the cottage leave the track and walking straight ahead over a grassy path reach a gate.

The gate bears a yellow arrow which denotes this is a public footpath.

If it had displayed a blue arrow this would have denoted a public bridleway. A public footpath is a legal route which can be travelled by foot. A bridleway is a legal route which can be travelled by foot, horseback or pedal cycle. These are both statutory rights of way. However, you may come across what is known as a 'permissive path'. These are paths which you may use by courtesy of the local landowner. They have no legal status and their use can be revoked at any time.

Pass through the gate and continue along the path climbing the slope of Loundon Hill. At first there is a plantation to your left but this soon ends to be replaced by a wire fence which accompanies you for a while before it angles away off to the left.

On the ascent of Loundon Hill, some 100m after passing the end of the plantation, the remains of an ancient settlement can be seen to the left of the path.

Remain on the path as it crosses the broad top of Louden Hill providing some grand views of the countryside ahead. After crossing the top the path descends to meet a red stone track. At the track turn right and on to pass through a gate. After about 160m leave the track, turning right on to a grassy path which climbs a slight rise.

At the top of this rise the buildings of Puncherton can be seen below and to your left. Puncherton is a sheep stock farm raising mostly Black Faced and Cheviot sheep.

The path descends into a shallow valley fording a burn at its foot and rising back up again. Keep to the path until you encounter a wire fence where you pass through a gate. Bear half-left to cross rough pasture finally reaching a gate set in a stone wall. Go through the gate and turn half-left to descend a slight slope crossing some 'inbye' land to reach a red stone track.

Inbye land is improved grass pasture near to a farm. This is good quality nutritious land on which the farmer grazes his cows, horses and sheep at lambing time. Outbye land is rough pasture away from the farm on which sheep graze for the most part of the year.

At the track turn right and pass through Puncherton farm, via gates bearing marker arrows. At the last gate turn left and descend a slope. There is a deep narrow valley to your right. At the foot of the slope pass through a gate in a wire fence and on a few steps to reach the Puncherton Burn.

The Puncherton Burn is a tributary feeding into the River Coquet further down the valley. Grey and Pied Wagtails frequent the many burns within the Cheviots.

Ford the burn and continue up a grassy path which climbs Rookland Hill. When you reach the top the path levels out and crosses the summit plateau

of the hill. Occasional wooden marker posts guide feet whilst on the summit keeping you on the right track. Soon a wire fence appears coming in from your left before running parallel to the path. At a stile set in the fence, cross the fence and looking ahead towards the ruins of Old Rookland make your way towards them.

Old Rookland is now a deserted farm steading. These abandoned cottages found littering the hills have usually been left to ruin because they did not have access to mains services or bus routes. Most of the shepherds of today find homes a long way from shops and schools unacceptable and with the advent of 'quad bikes' unnecessary.

Pass to the right of the farm ruins and continue through a gate. Follow the good grassy track keeping a stone wall on your left. The path soon veers to the right away from the wall and descends a slight slope to pass through a gap in a stone wall. After a few steps the Rookland Burn crosses your path and though presenting few difficulties must be forded.

The dry stone walls found throughout the Cheviots are generally of a double wall design. Two outer walls are built leaning slightly inwards with a space between. The space is filled with smaller stones. The walls average 1.75m in height to prevent sheep climbing over, not always successfully as sheep can be very agile.

Once across the burn follow a broad track which curves to the right, whilst climbing, to reach a gate. Go through the gate and remain on the track as it continues to climb and reach the summit of the hill. After crossing the summit plateau the track descends to meet a red stone track. Turn right on the track to continue descending and reach a wire fence. Pass through the gate and continue as the track gently curves to the right to reach another gate. Pass through this gate and on to a surfaced road. Turn left along this road to return to your starting point.

44. Prendwick to Ingram and Chesters

A walk comprising of a gentle climb and level most of the way, the return being downhill.

Distance: 13.6km (8½ miles)

Grade: Easy

Maps: Ordnance Survey Landranger 81. Ordnance Survey Pathfinders 487 NT81/91 and 488 NU01/11. Outdoor Leisure 16.

Start: Side of road, next to Prendwick Farm, GR003122.

Walk down to the farm and follow the road as it bends right and then left to descend into a dip. At the bottom of the dip is a signpost for Ingram. Pass through the gate and turn right to follow a strong track which runs parallel to trees on your right. Continue on the track as moves left away from the trees and climbs gently to reach a fork in the track. Take the right fork to a gate in a wire fence. Pass through and continue ahead over a grassy path which contours the side of Cochrane Pike until you reach a wire fence.

As the way climbs the view to the east expands with north Northumberland spread out below.

Once again go through the gate and follow the path which now travels along the side of Wether Hill to curve and start descending towards the hamlet of Ingram. Remain on the path to pass through further gates to reach a final gate leading on to a surfaced road. Turn right and follow the road as it bends left to reach the National Park Information Centre.

It is well worth visiting the centre. There is an exhibition room and a shop. The shop sells light refreshments and drinks as well as a good selection of books and brochures. The Church of St Michael to the side of the Centre has parts which are of Norman origin.

To the left of the car parking area a well-marked footpath leads through trees to reach another car park. At this car park turn left along the surfaced road and turn right to pass through Ingram. The road continues over a cattle grid and alongside a plantation. At the end of the plantation there is a signpost bearing directions for Chesters and Alnhammoor. Leave the road and follow

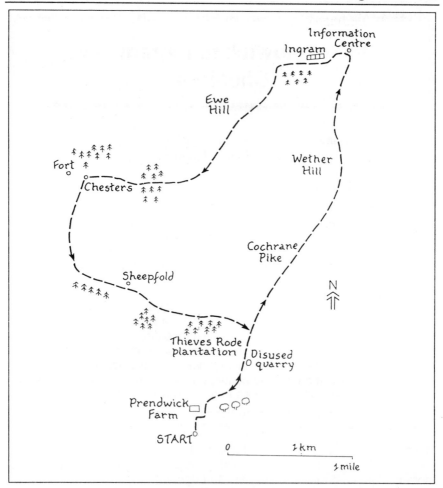

a track which rises up a hill. Just before the top there is a division of the track. Take the right-hand path which continues to rise reaching a white tipped marker post on level ground above. A dozen paces past the post turn right and follow a well-defined path which contours the side of Ewe Hill, climbing gently.

Below to your left can be seen an abandoned shepherd's cottage. These abandoned cottages one finds littering the hills were usually left because they did not have access to services or bus routes. As you climb, some trees will gradually enter your line of vision on the skyline ahead. This is where you are heading for.

At a white tipped marker post the path divides. Take the left path and a dozen paces on the path divides again. This time take the right-hand path. Walk on to reach the trees you saw earlier as you climbed Ewe Hill. Just before the trees there is a crossroads of paths. The correct route lies straight ahead towards a gate in the wire fence next to the plantation.

The trees are enclosed within a large square stone wall. They mostly comprise of a mixture of ash, elder and beech with an occasional Scots pine. You may occasionally see a large rabbit like creature hereabouts. It is not a big rabbit but a hare. Hares live above ground and have longer ears and legs and do not possess a white tail. They run rather than hop and when disturbed usually zig-zag across the open ground as a means of avoiding capture.

Cross the wire fence using the stile situated next to the gate and continue across a field to reach another get set in a wire fence visible on the skyline ahead. Cross via the stile. The path travels half-left. When you reach the point where the path forks take the minor path leading off to the right, curving around the slope of a hill. To your right can be seen the house of Chesters.

Originally a farm house it was later abandoned. In 1968 Whitley Bay Boy Scouts adopted it as an outdoor activities centre.

The path drops to a plantation set in a bowl shaped depression. A small gate allows you to enter the trees. After fording a small burn the path climbs through coniferous trees alongside a small burn to another gate allowing you to leave the plantation. Ahead can be seen Chesters. Walk towards it until you encounter a stone wall with a wire fence. Turn left here and follow next to the wall to reach a gate. Go through and along a path which takes you behind Chesters to another gate. pass through and on to a red stone track. Walk on for some 30 metres to reach a marker post. Turn right here and cross grass to reach the site of Chesters hill fort.

Chesters hill fort is located in a position which allows it to command an impressive view over the surrounding land. Ramparts and traces of hut circles are clearly visible.

Return to the marker post and turn right to follow the stone track up a slight rise to reach a wire fence. Go through the gate and walk on until just before a coniferous plantation the track bends to the right. Here, leave the track and continue straight ahead over a grass path to reach a fence running across the path from a plantation to your right.

You may well hear a loud 'curlee cur-lee' as you cross this stretch. This is the haunting cry of the curlew the bird with the long curving beak which lends itself as symbol to the Northumberland National Park. Its lone cry typifies this land of wide open spaces.

Pass through the gate and along a track parallel to the plantation. At the end of the plantation the track continues descending towards a burn before climbing up a hill side. At the top of the hill the path encounters a stone wall, with a plantation to the right. Pass through the gate in the wall.

Ahead and below, there is a panoramic view of the surrounding countryside and the Vale of Whittingham. On the skyline can be seen the outlines of the Simonside Hills above Rothbury. The small hamlet seen below is that of Prendwick.

There are a number of paths from the gate, the correct path turns half-left and follows a broad track which curves around a slope to pass above a mixed plantation underplanted with rhododendrons.

Rhododendrons are not native plants to this country. They were introduced during Victorian times and originated from the Himalayas. A large collection of rhododendrons can be viewed at the Hirsel Country Park, near Coldstream, previously the home of Sir Alec Douglas Home.

Continue through a gate and along the top of a coniferous plantation which adjoins it. The path passes this plantation before crossing open ground to a wire fence. Turn right here and through a gate. Continue descending to reach a broad track. Turn right and follow the track to return to Prendwick and your starting point.

45. Prendwick Circular

A gentle walk following an old highway before venturing into the lowland hills.

Distance: 9km (5½ miles)

Grade: Easy

Maps: Ordnance Survey Landranger 81. Ordnance Survey Pathfinder 488 NU01/10. Ordnance Survey Outdoor Leisure 16.

Start: East side of road next to Prendwick Farm GR003122. Please park considerately.

Walk to the farm and follow the road as it bends right and then left to descend into a dip. At the bottom of the dip there is a metal gate bearing a sign 'Path to Ingram 3½ miles'. Pass through the gate and on to a stony track which bends right and fords a narrow burn. Continue, climbing gently and parallel with the trees to your right. At the crest of the rise you will come to a fork in the track. Take the right-hand fork and continue to a metal gate. Pass through this gate and remain on the track with trees to your right. The track curves left away from the trees and rises to pass to the left of an old quarry.

This track was originally the old highway between Prendwick and the village of Ingram in the Breamish valley. The old quarry is one of many which can be found within the Cheviots. Rock extracted from them is used as material for sheep folds, stone walls and buildings.

Continue past the quarry with the track rising to reach another fork in the track. Take the left fork climbing a short slope to reach a wire fence. Go through the gate and follow a broad grassy path which takes you to the right of a plantation and then parallel to it. At a gate across the path go through and walk on as the path gradually curves to the right and away from the trees.

The plantation has the unusual name of Thieves Road Plantation. In the 14th century this path was a well-used route for joining up with Salters Road and crossing the Border ridge into Scotland.

The path rises gently to a gate set in a stone wall. Pass through the gate and to the right of a coniferous plantation before descending towards a burn.

This is the Leafield Burn. Along burns such as this, a popular bird is the Dipper. Easily identified by its white breast and short tail. Its startling habit is to fly into the water with wings outstretched, often emerging with a small fish in its beak.

Cross the burn then climb a slight slope to pass to the right of another

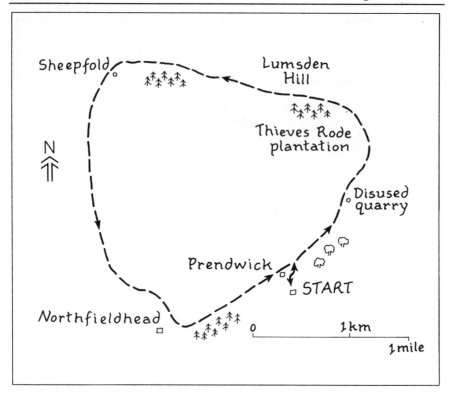

coniferous plantation. At a fork, take the right-hand branch and walk on for about 100m to reach a gate in a wire fence. Go through the gate and on a few steps to reach a stone farm track. Turn right along this track and follow it for 60m to reach a grass path leading away left from the track. Leave the track here and follow the path as it descends to a burn. Ford the burn and continue on a broader path which leads you to the left corner of a plantation.

The plantations within the Cheviots are mainly composed of coniferous trees. In 1919, after a serious depletion of the country's timber supply during the first World War, the Forestry Commission was set up with the task of replenishing the forests and ensuring a good reserve of timber for future needs.

At the corner of the plantation turn sharp left and, keeping a wire fence to your right make your way uphill for 200m before veering half-left and following an indistinct path which rises contouring the left side of the hill ahead.

The path is not clear on the ground. If in doubt aim to pass well to the left of the top of the hill, say about halfway up the side.

After rounding the hill the path continues over rough ground for 1km to reach a wire fence. At the fence turn left and walk alongside it to reach a gate. Pass through the gate and follow a broad farm track which first curves left and then curves right going around the side of Hart Law.

Once again difficulties can be encountered over this stretch. I would advise you to keep the wire fence to your right at a distance of around 300m and walk parallel to it. Eventually you will reach the wire fence as mentioned above. Below, there is the spread of the fertile fields of the Vale of Whittingham. It seems strange to think that some 300 million years ago this was one vast shallow sea.

At a wooden marker post beside the track turn left and descend as indicated. After 150m turn left to leave the track and follow a grass path which leads through bracken to rejoin the track at the bottom of the descent. Turn left along the track and continue as it bends right to reach a gate. Pass through and continue down a broad farm track with a line of trees to your left.

The buildings seen to your right are those of Northfieldhead.

Once through the next gate continue as the track bends left and takes you along a straight track with trees to your right and pasture land to your left. The track continues on for just over a kilometre to reach Prendwick Farm. At the farm turn left and then right through the farm buildings to exit on to the main road and the start of your walk.

Northumbrian sheep fold ('stell')

46. Shillmoor to Saughty Hill circular

A delightful walk up a quiet valley and back over the hills.

Distance: 9.2km (5¾ miles)

Grade: Moderate

Maps: Ordnance Survey Landranger 80. Pathfinders 487 NT81/91 and 499 NT80/90. Outdoor Leisure 16.

Start: Road verge before the bridge spanning the River Coquet GR886075.

Cross over the bridge spanning the River Coquet and turn right down the surfaced road leading towards the buildings of Shillmoor. After passing two houses on your left you will come to a notice board to the left of the road.

This bears the notice 'Ministry of Defence. Private road. No vehicles will be taken beyond this point except by authorised persons'.

Turn sharp left here to leave the road and proceed along a stony track which rises and curves to the left crossing a cattle grid. Remain on the track as it takes you up the valley with the Usway Burn flowing to your right. Pass to the left of a sheep fold and across another cattle grid. At a dark green coloured bridge spanning the burn cross over. Still further up the valley another two similar bridges also have to be crossed. After crossing the last bridge the track curves left and the buildings of Batailshiel Haugh can be seen ahead. Pass by a sign reading 'Out of bounds to military traffic' and on to cross a cattle grid. At the stone wall surrounding Batailshiel Haugh do not pass through the gate. Turn right to follow a permissive path which takes you around the perimeter of the farm.

The word 'shiel' as in Batailshiel means summer pastures. In Medieval times it was common practice for shepherds to graze their sheep on the higher hills during the summer and then move them down to lower land when winter came. Shiels were temporary dwellings for the summer months. Generally they were stone built with two rooms and a turf covered roof.

After passing the farm, ford a narrow burn and climb the bank following a grassy path. Keep a wire fence to your left until you reach a marker post bearing a blue arrow to the side of the path. Turn right and follow a tractor path which dips down to ford a burn. Remain on the track as it climbs a hill to reach

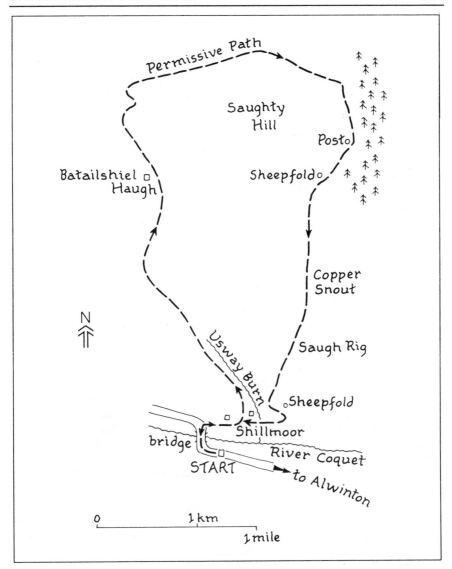

to reach a wire fence. Pass through a gate in the fence and remain on the track as it curves to the right of the summit of the hill to meet another gate in a wire fence. Pass through and keep to the track as it takes you across the top of the hill ahead before descending gently towards a forest road running along the side of the coniferous plantation visible ahead. At the road turn right.

You are now on Clennell Street. This was an old trading route stretching 19km from Alwinton to Hownam in Scotland. It was used by pedlars, drovers, reivers and smugglers.

Walk down the road for about 500 metres to reach a wooden marker post to the right of the road. Turn right and follow a grassy path to the corner of the plantation ahead. At the corner turn right and walk alongside the fence to reach a gate. Opposite, ther is a sheep fold to your right. Cross the stile next to the gate and follow a broad grassy path to the top of the hill.

To your right is the valley of the Usway Burn.

Valley of the Usway Burn

After crossing the top of the hill the path descends to meet a stone track. There is a wooden marker post to the right of the way. Turn right and descend a short distance before rising to the top of a low hill and a wire fence. Pass through the gate and continue to descend. The buildings of Shillmoor become visible ahead. The track bends to the left to pass to the right of a sheep fold and a brick hut before bending right to descend to Shillmoor. Cross over the foot bridge spanning the Usway Burn and head left towards a gate to the left of the large barn. Pass through the gate and follow the surfaced road past the farm buildings and on to the start of your walk

47. Tow Ford to Chew Green

A walk steeped in Roman history.

Distance: 13km (8 miles)

Grade: Moderate

Maps: Ordnance Survey Landranger 80. Pathfinders 486 NT61/71 and 498 NT60/70. Ordnance Leisure 16.

Start: Verge of road east of Tow Ford GR762134.

From your chosen parking spot follow the surfaced road south crossing over a cattle grid. Some dozen metres on and to your left is a signpost marked 'Dere Street'. Turn left here as indicated and, leaving the surfaced road, follow a grassy path climbing quite steeply to reach the saddle between Longside Law on your left and Woden Law on your right.

Pause at the top to catch your breath and admire the view behind you. On the other side of the Towford Burn the ridges and earthworks of the Roman camp at Pennymuir can be plainly seen. It was established during Agricola's conquest of southern Scotland around 80 AD. It was here troops undergoing training on Woden Law were quartered. The camp could accommodate around 2000 men. On the summit of Woden Law there was a training camp with extensive earthworks. There was a mock up fort on the summit and the troops could practice attacking it and learning military tactics. Prior to the Roman occupation a Celtic Iron Age fort stood on the summit. Woden was the name of an ancient Norse god.

At the top turn right walking parallel to a stone wall on your left. Where the wall ends continue along the path as it skirts the top of a deep basin dropping away to your left before climbing Blackhall Hill. At a wire fence ignore the gate and continue to climb parallel with the fence to your right. On arriving at the top of Blackhall Hill pass through another gate in the fence. The path descends gently keeping parallel to the Border fence on your left.

Dere Street was a Roman road built around 80 AD. The completed road when it was finished ran from Teeside to Crammond on the Firth of Forth. In the 18th and 19th centuries it was used as a drove road. Today it is used as an excellent walking route.

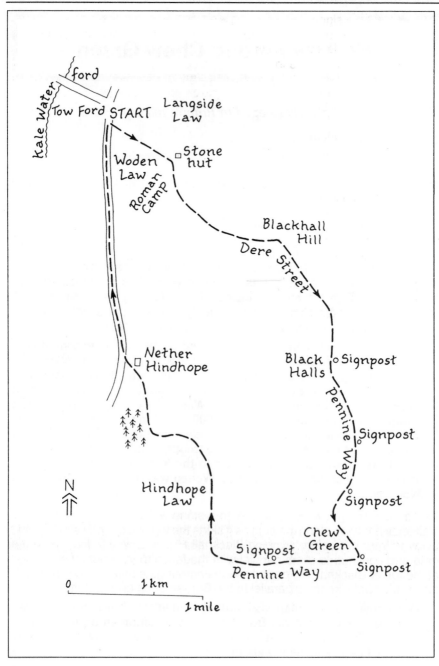

At a gate with a signpost next to it pass through the gate. Walk on with the Border fence to your right until you reach the next signpost. This informs you that Chew Green is a short distance ahead. Keep straight ahead on a broad grassy path and at a gate in a wire fence across your path cross via a stile to the right of it. Walk on until you reach a signpost and take the path to Chew Green as directed ahead. Marker posts guide your feet along. The path drops into a shallow gully before climbing up the other side. At the next marker post provided the path bends to the left taking you down to Chew Green itself visible as a network of ridges and earthworks to your right.

Chew Green was an extensive Roman camp built under the command of Agricola and used as a training camp, a long marching camp and also as a labour camp. In Medieval times this was the site of a settlement called Gamelspath. During the years of Border warfare in the 15th and 16th centuries it was appointed as a neutral meeting place where the Lords wardens of the Middle Marches could hold talks and attempt to sort out some of the local problems. In the 18th century cattle drovers would rest their herds overnight amongst the ridges.

At a four finger signpost ahead turn right and continue along the bottom edge of Chew Green now following the Pennine Way path. Pass a marker post and a few steps on cross a wire fence via the stile. Once over the stile ford

The remains of Chew Green Roman camp

the small burn before reaching another marker post. Climb the rise ahead making towards the signpost which becomes visible on the skyline ahead.

The signpost bears directions for the Pennine Way and Chew Green. The land over to your left is Ministry of Defence property and is used as a military training area.

Following the Pennine Way south arm walk on to reach a wire fence. Here, the path bends to the right and you continue with the fence on your left. At a wire fence across the way pass through the gate before bearing half-right along a grassy slope contouring the upper slope of the deep valley to your right. Later the path curves to the left and a tremendous view into Scotland opens up dramatically ahead.

Looking westward the view stretches to the distant Moffat Hills lining the horizon. The view encompasses most of the Borders Region with the television transmitter mast at Selkirk visible.

Continue on the path now descending and curving left to reach the top right corner of a coniferous plantation. A farm track takes you down the side of the trees and the farm buildings at Upper Hindhope to reach a surfaced road. Turn right and follow this road to pass the farm at Nether Hindhope. Continue on the surfaced road for 2.75km to return to your starting point at Tow Ford.